A Faith Fulfilled

Why Are Christians Across Great Britain Embracing Orthodoxy?

by Michael Harper

Conciliar Press
Ben Lomond, California

A Faith Fulfilled

First published in Great Britain 1997 by Hodder & Stoughton as *The True Light*

Library of Congress Cataloging-in-Publication Data

Harper, Michael, 1931–
[True light]
A faith fulfilled : why are Christians across Great Britain embracing Orthodoxy / by Michael Harper.
p. cm.
Includes bibliographical references.
ISBN 1-888212-12-8 (pbk.)
1. Harper, Michael, 1931– . 2. Orthodox Eastern converts—Great Britain—Biography. 3. Orthodox Eastern Church—Apologetic works. 4. Church of England—Controversial literature. 5. Orthodox Eastern Church—Great Britain—History—20th century. 6. Great Britain—Church history—20th century. I. Title.
BX747.9.H37A3 1998
248.2'4—dc21
[B] 98-13449
CIP

Dedicated
to the memory of
the Grand Duchess Elizabeth,
saint and martyr,
1864–1918

Table of Contents

Foreword

The thing I admire most about Michael Harper is not his love for Christ, his zeal to preach the gospel, or his loyalty to the Church. Many people carry these traits and I respect them deeply for that.

But with Father Harper, I admire most his courage. Few people I have met are willing to make the kinds of changes he has made because of his love for Christ, the gospel, and the Church. Or to say it more bluntly, Michael Harper has guts.

For years I had known him through his writings. Then, in the early 1990s, I met him on his journey to Orthodox Christianity. At his invitation, Father Michael Keiser, Father Bill and Dianna Olnhausen, and I were asked to visit England and to interact with hundreds of Christians—clergy and laity alike—concerning their desire to learn more about the Orthodox Faith.

Though the English are English and we Americans are American, the hunger for the fullness of the Faith on the part of our newly met brothers and sisters from Great Britain was not unlike the path of the thousands of us here who have become Orthodox in the last decade. And the one thing we tried to emphasize during our three-week visit to England was, "We are not here to import American Orthodoxy into England. We have come to bear witness to Christ and His Church that you may embrace this Faith in a British context."

Ultimately, Michael Harper, his devoted wife Jeanne, and numerous others said yes. And the Orthodox Church welcomed them home. This book is the captivating account of that historic transition.

Though a foreword to a book is generally not the place that one offers formal thanks, I will anyway. To His Beatitude,

IGNATIUS IV, Patriarch of Antioch; to His Eminence Metropolitan PHILIP, Primate of the Antiochian Orthodox Church in North America; and to His Grace, GABRIEL, Patriarchal Vicar for Western Europe (whom I have yet to meet)—thank you. For it was the arch-shepherds of Antioch who received us American evangelicals in the 1980s, and now, nearly a decade later, they stepped forward again to receive these willing pilgrims in Great Britain.

And perhaps the reason that we converts to Orthodoxy are so content to return home to the See of Antioch, where "the disciples were first called Christians" (Acts 11:26), is simply this: The courage of sojourners like Michael Harper to sell all for the pearl of great price is matched only by the courage of today's apostles of Antioch to keep alive the two-thousand-year-old tradition of evangelizing for Christ and receiving with open arms those who desire to enter this historic Church.

Fr. Peter E. Gillquist
Santa Barbara, California
Spring, 1998

Acknowledgments

My wife and I are grateful to God for the support we have received from so many people on our journey to Orthodoxy: those who helped us in the Pilgrimage to Orthodoxy, especially Archpriest Michael Keiser and Nicholas and Nina Chapman; our friends in the United States who encouraged us along the way, particularly Metropolitan PHILIP Saliba for his support at an early stage; Father Yves Dubois and the Greek Orthodox Community of Saint John of Kronstadt, Bath; Father Samir Gholam and the people of the Antiochian Orthodox Cathedral of Saint George, London; the priests and people of the British Antiochian Orthodox Deanery, who have shared this pilgrimage with us, especially Father Jonathan Hemmings for his careful reading of the typescript and his suggestions and improvements.

Above all we wish to thank His Beatitude IGNATIUS IV, the Patriarch of Antioch and all the East, and our Bishop, the Rt. Rev. GABRIEL Saliby, who welcomed us home and set up the British Antiochian Orthodox Deanery in 1995 to encourage and sustain us in the Orthodox way.

Introduction

Du, lieber Gott

These words—"To You, dear God"—were the last recorded words of the Grand Duchess Elizabeth, the one to whom this book is dedicated. She was born a princess in the German Royal Family, and Queen Victoria, with whom she frequently corresponded, was her grandmother. She was to die of starvation after being thrown down a disused mine shaft in Siberia on July 18, 1918, probably on the orders of Lenin. One of her biographers, E. M. Almedingen, writes that her last recorded words "must needs belong to history. Indeed He was her dear God. . . . No ideology would have meant anything to her; in those last moments nothing mattered except the will of God that offered the only absolute freedom to man."[1]

The false ideology of communism that caused her sudden and violent death is now a shadow of what it was then. Saint Elizabeth's faith and love live on. On that terrible day in 1918 they were a tiny flickering candle in the midst of great darkness; now theirs is a blazing light, joined to that of many others who also died for their faith, incarcerated in Lenin's and Stalin's gulags and Hitler's concentration camps.

The Grand Duchess Elizabeth was baptized a Lutheran. When she married Grand Duke Serge, the brother of Tsar Alexander III, she was put under no pressure by him, or by any other members of the Russian Royal Family, to convert to Orthodoxy. It was her own wish and decision to join the Russian Orthodox Church.

At an early stage on our pilgrimage my wife and I were given an icon of Saint Elizabeth. We hung it in a small prayer room we had. Later we moved it to another room when we converted it into a chapel. Her life has been a constant inspiration to us as we have made our own journey to Orthodoxy. Like Saint Elizabeth, we experienced no pressure either from the Church of England to stay or from the Orthodox Church to join it. It has been for us a personal decision, and our freedom to choose was respected. We are grateful for that.

Some may question whether a book such as this should be written, especially as we have been Orthodox for such a short time. I can understand such sentiments, but I believe there are good reasons for writing. The man who was born blind, after being healed by Jesus, refused to be drawn into theological discussions (see John 9:1–25). He was not qualified to make any contribution in that area. All he could say was, "One thing I know: that though I was blind, now I see." No one could argue with that statement. I am sure also that, so excited was he by his new sight, he saw things which others, who had always had their sight, missed.

This book is not a theological one. I am in no position to write such a book. It is the simple testimony, "I was blind but now I see." Perhaps in my enthusiasm for my new home in Orthodoxy I can see things that people who have been Orthodox all their lives have been missing.

A good definition of evangelism is "one beggar telling another beggar where to find bread." We are all beggars, entirely dependent on the grace and goodness of God. Part of that grace, for my wife and me, has been to find the Orthodox Church. Now we want to share with others our journey, and what we have found now that we are home.

1 *An Unbroken Unity,* Bodley Head, 1964, p. 137.

PART ONE

Becoming Orthodox

1

Coming Home

On behalf of the Church of Antioch we welcome you home to the Holy Orthodox Church. The Holy Synod has decided to receive the communities and people of the Pilgrimage to Orthodoxy into the Antiochian Patriarchate. . . . We give thanks to Almighty God for his mercy and kindness.

His Beatitude Patriarch Ignatius IV,
September 1994

"We welcome you home," said the Patriarch of Antioch to a group of Anglican priests gathered in our bishop's apartment in Paris in September, 1994. Our joy was complete. Our cups were running over. The suspense of the waiting period had ended. The doors were open, not only for us, but also for many lay people back in England who belonged to our parishes.

The words "welcome home" were music to our ears. They summed up our emotions. This was the fulfillment of our hopes. Like the prodigal son, we had been a long way from home; like him, we were not sure what our father would do when we came home. But our patriarch opened his arms to us like the father in the parable and invited us into the home of Orthodoxy.

The words were to find a new resonance for my wife and me on a cold and dull March morning in 1995 as we were led by Father Samir Gholam into the Orthodox Cathedral in London. The Celts had a special word for the desire for home—*hiraeth,* meaning an extreme yearning. We had experienced that too, and our yearnings were now fulfilled.

I don't know where moving from one church to another comes on the Richter scale of emotional disturbances. My guess is that it is pretty high. The Church of England is not an easy church to leave. Archbishop Fisher once said, "We have to love the Church of England because it is so completely English." So in a sense leaving meant losing part of our national heritage. It is still not easy for some people to think of the Orthodox or Roman Catholics as "British." Such thoughts are unfair to both groups, because Britain was Roman Catholic before it was Anglican, and Orthodox before it was Roman Catholic. Nevertheless, Orthodoxy, for most British people, seems to be an Eastern rather than a Western religion. It still appears to some like a foreign incursion, its churches out of place in England's green and pleasant land. The Church of England, by contrast, looks as if it was made to measure.

Another problem was my age. It is more difficult to make a radical change when one is in one's sixties than when one is younger. I was also getting lazy-minded, wanting to relax a bit after a busy life in which there had been many pressures. Retirement was beckoning. The cool evening breezes of life were beginning to have their appeal. I no longer wanted a place in the noonday sun, but yearned to do things I had never had the time to do before. I coveted a retirement mode of existence. New challenges were the last thing I wanted; I had had plenty of them already for one lifetime.

We had been Anglicans for over sixty years, and I had been a priest for nearly forty. It was hard to leave after such a long time, with so many happy memories and so many friends in that church. I struggled for a long time over it. Yet the journey home had started and had to be completed. There was no going back.

There is such a thing as a "conversion mentality"; I have observed it in some of my friends who have converted from one church to another. I suppose I must have it too, though I do guard against being overenthusiastic about the church we have joined and hypercritical about the one we have left. It is hard at first to get used to the new situation. However, as we move further and further from the epicenter of this emotional earthquake, we are acquiring an altogether wiser and more balanced perspective on the issues. My wife and I realize that we have left behind a church that has much to commend it. We also know that we have joined a church with faults, some quite serious.

Then there were friends to consider. Inevitably we were plagued by the thought, "I wonder what he or she will think about this." Or, "Will they still want to be friends?" We felt guilty also: "I have betrayed the Church of England." "I am an ungrateful son of the Church." "I have let them down." "They will not forgive me." Worst of all is the constant thought, "I am judging and condemning them by my actions." I am saying, in effect, "You have forced me to do this." In the end it was God's call to the Orthodox Church that was decisive. It was more important than anything. All else has paled into insignificance in the light of that call.

We "came home" on March 15, 1995. It was as if all that had gone before had been a preparation for that moment. By an uncanny coincidence, many of the important moments in my life have taken place close to the cathedral where we entered Holy Orthodoxy. My parents were married in a church less than a mile away. Three years later I was born in a nursing home just around the corner. On May 29, 1931, I was baptized in Saint Mark's Church, North Audley Street, and my first home was in Weymouth Street, near Saint George's Cathedral.

Many years later I was to put down strong evangelical roots as a curate in All Souls, Langham Place. This famous building, next to Broadcasting House, was the model for our Orthodox cathedral and almost within sight of it. It was there too that I had an experience of God the Holy Spirit that was to influence my life profoundly, leading me to devote a great part of my life to the charismatic renewal. In the 1950s I began courting a young student at the Royal Academy of Music, just down the road. Jeanne and I were married in 1956.

In the end it was the desire to know and follow the truth that was responsible for this radical decision, *for truth matters.* But I need to enter an important *caveat.* We can never possess the truth; it is always greater than are we and our finite understanding of it. It is the truth that possesses us. In this life, as Saint Paul says, "we see in a mirror, dimly" (1 Cor. 13:12). God is always greater than our poor grasp of the truth. As Michael Novak has said, "Truth leads us where it will. It is not ours for mastering."[1]

"Truth" is a small, five-letter word that, sadly, is greatly neglected today. Like Pontius Pilate, people ask a prior question, "What is truth?" and are not sure of the answer. But small though this word is, on it hangs a great deal, and to be captured by it is to find true meaning to life. Without it, life is empty and vain.

The decision, when it came to it, was not hard. The leaving, on the other hand, was difficult and painful. Our journey to Orthodoxy was often nail-biting and at times distressing. Truth has always been difficult to follow and embrace. Jesus Christ, our Lord and Savior, never hid from His disciples the cost of being faithful to the truth. Becoming Orthodox was not easy; yet we have had no regrets about what we did.

1 *Awakening from Nihilism: Why Truth Matters,* IEA, 1995, p. 15. This was the address given by him in Westminster Abbey on the occasion of his receiving the Templeton Prize.

2

Truth and New Ideas—A General Overview

> *The Elder, to the elect lady and her children, whom I love in truth, and not only I, but also all those who have known the truth, because of the truth which abides in us and will be with us forever: Grace, mercy, and peace will be with you from God the Father and from the Lord Jesus Christ, the Son of the Father, in truth and love.*
>
> *2 John 1–3*

In the passage quoted above, it is stated that the truth will be "with us" for ever; and that God's grace, mercy, and peace will be "with you" in truth and love. The divine title Immanuel means "God with us." It is, therefore, encouraging to know that not only God's grace but truth itself will be "with us" for ever. God and truth are one.

When you are a member of a church you have the right, and sometimes the duty, to draw attention to its failures, especially when it departs from the truth. Saint Athanasius, who was Bishop of Alexandria from 328 to 373, was not the most popular man in the Church at the time of his protests against Arius. Yet few would fail to recognize the supreme importance of what he did. Today there may be occasions when you need to take action in protest at what you believe to be your church's unfaithfulness. Like Saint Athanasius, you may find that this can be lonely, for you may be in a minority. Your stance may incur "exile," which he suffered on six occasions. But when you leave one church and move to another, you forfeit that right to protest. Your duties now lie with the new communion you have joined, and you are bound to act towards your former church with courtesy and grace. The Church of England, in our case, has forgiven us much; we must forgive also.

Without contradicting what has just been written, I do owe it to my readers to explain why a lifelong Anglican would consider moving to another church. Clearly, in my eyes, there were faults in Anglicanism, some so serious they at first made me restless and then forced me to look in other directions. I wish to point out these faults (in chapter 3) without bitterness and as fairly as possible.

The Church of England has fine qualities, and I still have many friends in it. During my lifetime it has produced outstanding scholars like Archbishop Michael Ramsey, Dr. Eric Mascall, and Dr. Austin Farrer. The evangelical world has been enriched by Anglicans like Dr. John Stott and Dr. James Packer. The great apologist C.S. Lewis was an Anglican. Throughout the nearly five hundred years of its history, the Church of England has nurtured outstanding saints and scholars, apologists and missionary pioneers. To leave such a great heritage could never be easy.

In the 1960s a well-known Roman Catholic theologian, Dr. Charles Davis, a Jesuit at Heythrop College, left the Roman Catholic Church. He wrote a book called *A Question of Conscience* (Hodder & Stoughton, 1967) in which he commented, "I need to write a book to get my bearings. But I also owe others a full account of my present convictions" (p. 13). When I read the book, it left a bad taste in my mouth. Was the Roman Catholic Church really as bad as all that? I think not. Probably the book was written too soon after the events that led to his leaving. I do not wish to make the same mistake. I am not writing this book "to get my bearings." You don't have to write books to do that. However, I am writing it, as Dr. Davis did his, so that others can fully understand why we took these steps. We owe this especially to those who know us and are puzzled by our actions.

Conscience is a delicate part of our human make-up. It needs to be educated and can at times be conditioned by cultural factors. While one person may do something "as a question of conscience," another may take a different course of action—even do the opposite. It is unfortunate that we live in a day when consciences are not as tender or as well educated as they once were.

We have also to appreciate that throughout history the church has been involved in endless controversy, and our day is no exception. Cardinal Ratzinger, one of the pillars of the Roman Catholic Church, is today the doyen of Catholic orthodoxy. Yet that was not always the case. For a long time he was a close friend and associate of the radical Dr. Hans Küng. Then he changed. He saw that the new ideas conflicted with the old. He was no longer able to bear it. These words describe my experience too: I was no longer able to bear the new ideas. For Ratzinger it was a change of position within the same church; for us it meant moving to another church. Many church people face the same dilemma. There are so many "new ideas" circulating. These can ultimately destroy our belief and confidence even in a church of which we may have been members since the cradle.

The Protestant churches in Western Europe and North America are in deep crisis; they are literally dying out. The well-known Protestant theologian of the University of Munich, Wolfhart Pannenberg, has said, "Only Roman Catholic, Orthodox and evangelical Protestant churches will survive the twenty-first century unless mainline Protestant churches stop wavering in their faith and Christian identity." As reported in the World Council of Churches newspaper *One World* (Aug./

Sept. 1994), Dr. Pannenberg accused Protestant churches of "surrendering the substance of the Christian faith." He went on to say, "Protestant churches are in acute danger of disappearing if they continue neither to resist the spirit of the progressively secularist culture nor to try to transform it."

The Background of Concern

Dr. Pannenberg has raised important questions, and we need to look carefully at the way the truth is approached in our Western culture. We will see that the *thinking* of Western churches has come to have more in common with secular thought than with biblical and traditional Christian thought. Churches in the West are eager to be relevant to the fashions of thought, mores, and standards of modern society; sometimes this desire is combined with the hope that it will draw people to the Church. Yet the primary role of the Church is to please *God* and be relevant to *Him,* not to people.

Dr. Samuel Johnson once wrote about the people of his day and their desire to be fashionable, "The greatest part of mankind has no other reason for their opinions than that they are in fashion." For many years trendiness has been a driving force in Western Christianity, sometimes going to absurd lengths. Churches are often dogmatic in areas like politics and economics, where God has not always revealed Himself plainly and where a variety of opinions is usually healthy. At the same time churches are increasingly indecisive about fundamental doctrinal and moral issues concerning which God's truth and laws are plainly revealed.

I want to enlarge on this by referring to three high-profile words that are often used generally today and are increasingly used by the media—pluralism, relativism, and subjectivism. They need careful definition. What do these current buzzwords mean?

Pluralism

This was originally used to describe the condition of bishops or priests who held more than one office at a time. It is still used in the Church of England in connection with a priest who has more than one benefice or parish at the same time. I am not considering the term in that sense. It has also come to be used in a secular sense to describe societies that have several different religious, racial, or ethnic groups. Thus British society is often now spoken of as a pluralistic society. I am not using the word in this social sense either. (I have always supported human rights for those who are either racially or ethnically different from myself. In that sense I have always been a pluralist.)

I am using the term "pluralism" to refer to a way of *thinking,* not to a way of *living.* The *Oxford English Dictionary* describes it as a system of thought or philosophy that "recognises more than one ultimate principle." It is *religious* and *intellectual* pluralism that is my concern here, and an obvious example would be the practice of multi-faith services. Here I am certainly not a pluralist. New Age is one of the most fertile soils in which pluralism thrives, but it is not the only one. Our age is far from being one of unbelief; rather, people today will believe *anything,* a state that Michael Novak calls "arrogant gullibility."[1]

Relativism

Relativism is the conviction that no ideas or beliefs are universally true; all are relative, and their validity depends on circumstances. Michael Novak has called this way of thinking "an invisible gas, odourless, deadly, which is now polluting every free society on earth."[2] It acts like the tear gas used by police forces. It paralyzes consciences and weakens moral fiber. For modern man relativism means that there is no such thing as truth; there are only opinions, yours and mine, and you can take your pick.

Here is a strange example of relativism gone mad. Some American academics have tried to prove that the roots of Western civilization lie not in Greece or Israel, but in Africa. Thus "Afro-centric" teachers conclude that Greece was a colony of Egypt and that Socrates was black. A classical scholar, Mary Lefkowitz, has exposed this form of relativism in her book, *Not Out of Africa.* She has had to face great opposition, including the accusation that she is a racist. She has described her fight as against "relativism, lack of respect for the truth, and the abuse of learning for political purposes."[3] This leads us to the third ingredient of this dangerous trio of modern ideas.

Subjectivism

Subjectivism means that the ultimate test of what is true is how we feel, or what we experience, rather than what is true according to objective reality. "If it feels good, do it," is a modern way of expressing the moral dimension of the term. C.S. Lewis wrote a famous essay that he called, "The Poison of Subjectivism,"[4] and that is exactly what it is. In the essay Lewis draws our attention to the fact that after studying his environment, man has begun to study himself. His own reason has now become the object of study: "It is as if we took out our own eyes to look at them."[5] When logic becomes merely subjective, Lewis writes, "there is no reason for supposing it yields truth." The well-known Anglican convert to the Roman Catholic Church, Ronald Knox, once put it this way:

> . . . When suave politeness
> Tempering bigot zeal
> Corrected "I believe"
> To "one does feel" . . .

Today personal opinion is often confused with faith. What I personally believe, however crazy, is "my faith." Dom Gregory

Dix once said, "The opposite of faith is not doubt; it is personal opinion." Most people in our Western world believe that all religions are equally valid (pluralism); that all truth is relative, never absolute (relativism); and that our beliefs and our behavior are determined primarily by how we feel, what we experience, and the circumstances or the "situation" we are in (subjectivism). Most people still believe in "God," but not in a God who has revealed Himself to us as ultimate truth or one with ultimate sanctions relating to moral behavior. So we make up our beliefs as we go along. We adjust our behavior according to our own choice or circumstances, not according to any divine or moral absolutes.

The Death of Truth

A recent book on the Victorians carries the title *The Demoralisation of Society* (IEA Health and Welfare Unit, 1995). The author, Gertrude Himmelfarb, traces the decline of society "from Victorian Virtues to Modern Values." She writes, "It is not until the present century that morality became so thoroughly relativised and subjectified that virtues ceased to be 'virtues' and became 'values'. This transmutation is the great philosophical revolution of modernity, no less momentous than the earlier revolt of the 'Moderns' against the 'Ancients'—modern science and learning against classical philosophy" (p. 9).

The "death of God" has led swiftly to the death of morality and the death of truth. Gertrude Himmelfarb puts it well: "There would be no good and evil, no virtue and vice; there would be only 'values'" (p. 10). The world has always concocted its own mix of poisons, and our day is no different from all others since the dawn of creation. In the beginning Adam and Eve believed the lies of Satan rather than the word of God.

As we have seen, Western thinking is nowadays permeated by pluralism, relativism, and subjectivism. Pablo Picasso described the art of painting as the work of a blind man: "He paints not what he sees, but what he feels and what he tells himself about what he has seen."[6] In other words, you respond not to what you *see* but to what you *feel.* Or, as he put it on another occasion, "An artist must know how to convince others of the truth of his lies."

But there are people who paint what they see. Roseanne Skoke, the Liberal Member of Parliament for Central Nova, Canada, for example, writing in the January 1996 issue of the Canadian magazine *Citizen,* has spotted these mental viruses. She writes, referring to pluralism and relativism:

> They make no allowance for *truth.* Truth has been replaced by relativism, which seeks to legitimise diverse choice . . . so truth becomes nothing more than personal opinion. Relativism in our pluralistic society has stripped us of our ethical and moral guidelines. . . . Pluralists and relativists consider morality *passé.* They reject absolute moral truths and replace them with the theory of individualist freedom of choice . . . the silence of the Church is almost deafening . . . why has it abandoned its role, and surrendered its duty of moral persuasion and influence?

Another writer who is asking the same question is Lord Rees-Mogg. Writing in *The Times* (Dec. 11, 1995), he once described the Church of England as "riddled with relativism." He goes on, "and there is too much of it in the Roman Catholic Church, despite the Pope."

We have lived through a century in which truth has become what we feel and experience rather than ultimate reality. So people want a God whom they can make in their own image, rather than allowing their carnal natures to be changed painfully to become like His. They want a church their size and shape, to fit their mind and thoughts, not one shaped by God and His mind and thoughts. We have become a generation of idolaters, not worshippers of the true God. G.K. Chesterton once wrote of his generation, "We are on the road to producing a race of men too mentally modest to believe in the multiplication table."

Defenders of the Faith

A close friend of ours, who died suddenly in October, 1994, epitomized passion for the truth. He was typical of many Anglican lay people who are confused and hurt by the follies of some leaders. Yet they are loyal to the church and possess an instinct for the truth which refuses to accept the perversions of it in the modern church. Such people cannot always give the reasons why, but they know with inner conviction when someone crosses the line and trespasses in heretical territory.

In my funeral address I called this friend "Mr. Valiant-for-Truth" (the name of a character in John Bunyan's *Pilgrim's Progress*). My friend Monty had suffered deeply as he saw the Church of England lurch from one crisis of faith to another. The Apostle John, who was truly "Mr. Valiant-for-Truth," once wrote, "To the beloved Gaius, whom I love in truth" (3 John 1). Monty was a member of the band of truth-lovers, like Gaius and so many others. John Stott, in his commentary on the epistles of Saint John, expresses it well: "the truth being the sphere in which their [Saint John's and Gaius's] mutual love existed and flourished." Later he writes about Gaius, "He was a balanced Christian. He held the truth in love. He loved in truth . . . he was a transparent, open Christian who was letting his light shine and not hiding it under a bushel."[7]

God is seeking today people like this to combat the lies and half-truths that are rising like a thick fog to obscure the faith. Yet it is not a new problem; the early Christians faced similar situations. "I found it necessary to write to you," says Jude, "exhorting you to contend earnestly for the faith which was once for all delivered to the saints" (Jude 3). And the Apostle John writes often about this in his letters. He has been called "the Apostle of love," but he was also "the Apostle of truth." The word "truth" occurs no fewer than twenty times in these letters.

Truth for John was both doctrinal (what we believe) and moral (how we behave). Truth is about something we *do* as well as something we believe in. The Orthodox writer A.M. Coniaris has written, "Christianity is much more than a creed: it is a deed, a life to be lived . . . creeds and deeds go together."[8] Saint John makes the moral aspect of truth clear when he writes, "If we say that we have no sin, we deceive ourselves, and the truth is not in us" (1 John 1:8; see also 2:4). So truth concerns fraud, corruption, dishonesty, homosexuality, adultery, cohabitation, abortion, and other issues for which the Protestant churches seem to have no clear message. It also concerns the Incarnation and the nature of Christ, the Trinity, the Cross and the Resurrection, and other doctrines that are part of the Apostles' teaching from the first century.

In his second letter John writes to the "elect lady." Many believe this was a church rather than an individual woman. He says of her that he loves her "in truth . . . because of the truth which abides in us and will be with us forever" (2 John 1, 2). This was why we became Orthodox, because of the *truth,* which is the only sure foundation for the Church of Jesus Christ.

Saint John goes on to treat love and truth as partners. We are to walk both "in truth" (v. 4) and in love (v. 6). It is not simple to do both at the same time. When we focus on truth, it is easy to be harsh, judgmental, and dogmatic. When we focus on love, we tend to be sentimental. An obsession with truth can make us narrow and sectarian. Love without the underpinning of truth can make us woolly-minded to the point of being religious and intellectual pluralists.

I fear that the tendency these days is to go for love at the expense of truth. Yet without truth, love lacks the biblical balance that is so clearly witnessed to by the Apostles and, later, the Church Fathers. Saint John is not afraid, if necessary, to name troublemakers (3 John 9). He is quite prepared to call the enemies of the truth "antichrist" (2 John 7). He refers to the "evil deeds" of some (2 John 11) and tells the church people not to welcome false teachers into their homes (2 John 10). Strong words!

Truth and Unity

Another major concern today is Christian unity, and this is most welcome. The divisions in the Church are a scandal and a hindrance to the spreading of the gospel message. Yet we need to be reminded that in the great prayer of Jesus for unity in John 17, He refers to truth *first;* He says, "Sanctify them by Your truth. Your word is truth" (v. 17). Only then does He pray for unity: "that they may be one . . . that they may be made perfect in one" (vv. 22, 23). Sadly, the truth factor can so easily be marginalized or left out altogether in the quest for unity. But unity without agreement on truth will be illusory and will lack true value. It will be unity of the lowest common denominator.

Dr. Graham Leonard (formerly the Anglican Bishop of London, now a priest in the Roman Catholic Church), writing in the *Church of England Newspaper* ("Directions," June, 1993), said, "We live in a time when the order is reversed. Instead of living under the judgment of the truth revealed in Christ, which is the basis of true unity . . . truth is, it is supposed, to be discovered and expressed by what is thought to be acceptable to the mind of a particular generation."

Truth and Conscience

Finally, truth needs to be linked with conscience, as we see it expressed in the teaching of the Apostle Paul. When he writes to Timothy, he is aware, even at this early stage of the Church's development, that the truth is under threat. So he urges the younger leader to hold on to "faith and a good conscience, which some having rejected, concerning the faith have suffered shipwreck" (1 Tim. 1:19), and to hold "the mystery of the faith with a pure conscience" (1 Tim. 3:9). In these two passages Saint Paul writes in the same breath of a good conscience and truth, and we too need to join them together. Conscience is about not only what we do but also what we believe.

It is a striking fact that the phrase that occurs more often than any other on the lips of Christ in the four Gospels (no fewer than eighty-one times) is "Amen, Amen," often translated as, "I tell you the truth." It is that truth and that faith that Jude declares was "once for all delivered to the saints." Truth is God's, not ours, and it is his by inalienable right. To pursue the truth is our divine calling, from which we must never turn back.

The period we have recently passed through has not been conducive to such a faithful pursuit of God's truth. It has been unfashionable to claim to know the truth. In his trial before the Roman governor, Jesus Christ affirmed, "Everyone who is of the truth hears My voice" (John 18:37), to which the Roman governor retorted cynically, "What is truth?" In the words of Francis Bacon, "He would not stay for an answer." Today there are many who question whether "truth" is a word fit for use in the English language. Some question whether it means anything at all and whether it can be treated seriously.

Mix 'n' Match

We live today in a world of "mix 'n' match." People will often, without any sensible criteria, select what they like from a variety of sources, even contradictory ones, and mix them together in a smorgasbord of ideas. There is a strong current flowing against dogmas of any kind, even the most simple and foundational. Confusion and ambiguities abound. Truth is seen as relative rather than absolute, plural rather than unique, general rather than particular, and arrived at subjectively rather than in the light of objective reality. People claim at last to have done what no previous generation has attempted: they have reconciled light and darkness, and married the sheep and the goats. Our attitude to truth is no longer like our relationship with our spouse, to whom we are committed in faithfulness and love for eternity, but like a series of temporary liaisons—lovers embraced and then discarded for the next partner of the moment. Truth has been prostituted by some, carelessly treated and trivialized by others. When you marry the spirit of the age, you are quickly widowed.

Rightly, today there is a distaste for rigid fundamentalism, especially that of terrorists who shoot people they disagree with and explode bombs in countries like Northern Ireland and Israel. Of that spirit there was not a trace in the lives of the saints, who always matched their love *for* the truth with their love *in* the truth. For them truth was not something arrived at easily. It was not a quick fix. They lived it and sometimes died for it; they prayed it, offered it at the Eucharist, and saturated their minds with it in the Scriptures and the works of the Fathers.

C.S. Lewis has made this point well in two extracts from the book *The Business of Heaven*:[9]

True or False?

One of the great difficulties is to keep before the audience's mind the question of Truth. They always think you are recommending Christianity not because it is *true* but because it is *good*. . . . You have to keep forcing them back, and again back, to the real point. Only thus will you be able to undermine . . . their belief that a certain amount of "religion" is desirable but one must not carry it too far. One must keep on pointing out that Christianity is a statement that, if false, is of *no* importance and, if true, of infinite importance. The one thing it cannot be is moderately important.

Defending the Faith

We are to defend Christianity itself, the faith preached by the apostles, attested by the martyrs, embodied in the creeds, expounded by the fathers. . . . The great difficulty is to get modern audiences to realise *that you are preaching Christianity solely and simply because you happen to think it is true;* they always suppose you are preaching it because you like it or think it is good for society or something of that sort. . . . This immediately helps them to realise that what is being discussed is a question about objective fact, not gas about ideals and points of view. . . .

Do not attempt to water down Christianity. There must be no pretence that you can have it with the supernatural left out. So far as I can see Christianity is precisely the one religion from which the miraculous cannot be separated. You must frankly argue for supernaturalism from the very outset.

A good example of the point that C.S. Lewis is making in these quotations is the famous singer Sir Cliff Richard, who became a Christian in 1960. A national newspaper reported that he was a Christian "not because he thinks Christianity 'exciting', 'relevant', or 'challenging', *but because he believes it to be true*" (my italics).

I realize that claiming to "know the truth" may seem proud to some and offensive, even arrogant, to others. Yet Jesus did say, "You shall know the truth, and the truth shall make you free" (John 8:32). And we will one day be judged according to the truth. In *Awakening from Nihilism,* Michael Novak has written, "Judgment Day is the truth on which civilisation is grounded." In the end we are under the judgment of the One "who is undeceivable." We will be judged not only by what we have done, but also by what we have believed and what we have taught.

I have discovered, since becoming Orthodox, an angle on this that I find compelling. If followed, it guarantees that we will not act like narrow-minded fundamentalists. The Eastern Church has always seen the nature of God as a "mystery." It has been less cerebral and, therefore, less dogmatic than the Western church. About some aspects of the Faith it is content to say, "It is a mystery," when the Western church has been inclined to define and categorize them.

The writer and former *Everyman* presenter Peter France has recently converted to the Orthodox Church. He writes about his conversion, "I feel the Western Church approach is too rational . . . in Eastern Christianity the ultimate reality is a mystery that you wouldn't attempt to articulate or rationalise" (*Sunday Telegraph,* September 1, 1996). An example of this would be the Eastern Church's lack of teaching on purgatory. It is reluctant to define rigidly what happens after death. For the Orthodox, truth is not a system of thought. Mother Maria of Normanby has written, "Truth is not created. Truth *is.* Christ *is* the Truth."[10]

Dr. Sheridan Gilley too makes the point in an article in the *Guardian* newspaper (April 14, 1993). He is explaining why he left the Anglican Church and became a Roman Catholic. "The theologian," he writes, "can do no more than try reason and experience to discern the mystery of God more deeply. Christianity is a truth to which the human mind is not equal. It is not a philosophy, though it has used a range of philosophies from Plato to existentialism to explain itself. And while the gospel is given through a culture, its message transcends culture. The liberal rationalises the mystery and thereby strains it away."

Dr. Gilley is a senior lecturer in theology at Durham University, so he saw and heard Bishop David Jenkins (about whom more in the next chapter) at close quarters. I believe he expresses succinctly where Dr. Jenkins and those like him err. They attempt, as he has put it, to "rationalise the mystery." Such an approach can have dangerous and destructive effects on Christian faith.

The descriptions of the pilgrim's journey in *Pilgrim's Progress* are particularly appropriate for those seeking to follow the ways of truth. The truth-seeker may have to visit Doubting Castle and meet Giant Despair. He will frequent the Delectable Mountains and the Slough of Despond. The pilgrim will have carefully to avoid Vanity Fair and the water-man, who looks one way and rows another. The serious Christian will do battle with Apollyon in his prayers. Above all, Mr. Valiant-for-Truth must never allow discouragement

To make him once relent
His first avow'd intent
To be a pilgrim.

1 *Awakening from Nihilism: Why Truth Matters,* p. 19.
2 Ibid.

3 Article by Michael Gore, *The Times,* 2 September 1996.
4 Published in *Christian Reflections,* ed. Walter Hooper, Bles, 1967, pp. 72–81.
5 Ibid., p. 72.
6 From the chapter entitled "Childhood" in Jean Cocteau's *Journals.*
7 *Tyndale New Testament Commentaries,* Tyndale Press, 1964, pp. 218, 219.
8 *Orthodoxy: A Creed for Today,* Light and Life Publishing, 1972.
9 Ed. Walter Hooper, Collins, 1984, pp. 30–31.
10 Quoted by Bishop Kallistos Ware in *The Orthodox Way,* St. Vladimir's Seminary Press, 1993, p. 113.

3

Truth and New Ideas— In the Anglican World

In the Church of England things are not always what they seem to be. Indeed the public perception of its character rarely corresponds to the reality of its working.
Opening sentences of the preface to Crockford's Clerical Directory, 1987/8

I have lived through a period in the life of the Church of England when, to paraphrase the words of the poet W.B. Yeats, things have fallen apart. It is ironic that around the ceiling of the Assembly Hall of Church House, Westminster, are the words, "Holy is the True Light." It is in this hall that things have fallen apart, especially on November 11, 1992, when the decision was taken to ordain women to the priesthood.

Although I did not realize it at the time, the journey to the Orthodox Church began in earnest for me when *The Myth of God Incarnate* was published in Britain in 1977.[1] The book raised a storm as soon as it reached the bookstores. The General Synod of the Church of England condemned it. A *Church Times* headline referred to the authors as "seven against Christ." An Orthodox archbishop declared that the authors had "fallen prey to an opposition of a demonic character."

The second edition was published in 1993. In the new preface the editor, John Hick, wrote, "Within the scholarly world the central themes of the book had long been thoroughly familiar. The view that divine incarnation is a metaphorical or mythic idea is in fact widespread even when [its proponents] are regarded as defenders of traditional orthodoxy" (pp. x–xi). He then quotes Dr. John Macquarrie as an example; Macquarrie was a contributor to a counter-blast book that was hurriedly edited by Canon Michael Green and called *The Truth of God Incarnate* (Hodder & Stoughton, 1977).

These words only serve to underline the confusion that exists on the one hand, and the widespread denial of this fundamental tenet of the Christian Faith on the other. It is interesting to learn what has happened to the contributors to *The Myth of God Incarnate* in the meanwhile. One (Michael Goulder) is now an atheist. Don Cupitt has moved to a position close to strands of Buddhism; he is the leader of a group called the Sea of Faith, consisting mostly of Anglican clergy, that denies virtually all the main tenets of the Christian Faith. Most of the others maintain the position they held when they contributed to the book, though one of them (Frances Young) has moved a little to the right.

When I studied theology at Cambridge University in the 1950s, I met and sat at the feet of those whose teaching was liberal, sometimes markedly so. Generally the men were humble, tentative, and respectful of the views of traditionalists like me. They never mocked the cherished beliefs of those who still stuck to the old ways and teachings. The book *Honest to God* (SCM, 1963), however, was to set a new trend. The author, Dr. John Robinson, then Bishop of Woolwich, wrote it in bed suffering from back problems. He begins the book with the statement, "I find myself a bishop at a moment when the discharge of this burden can seldom have demanded greater depth of divinity and quality of discernment, for we stand on the brink of a period in which it is going to become increasingly difficult to know what the true defence of Christian truth requires." He was right, and the publication, some fourteen years later, of *The Myth of God Incarnate* made this abundantly plain.

This book was a much more serious frontal assault on orthodoxy. It was written by the then avant-garde theologians. One of them (Dr. Maurice Wiles) was at the time chairman of the Doctrine Commission of the Church of England. Together with many of my friends, I was deeply disturbed. Were not the foundations of faith at stake?

Beauty or Ashes?

In 1979 I was invited to give the Ashe Lecture, and I chose for its title, "Beauty or Ashes?" (taken from Isaiah 61:3). The lecture, delivered on September 20, was an expression of my deep anxiety for my church and its response to destructive heterodoxy. I said in this lecture, "The disease has a terminal look about it . . . at the present time I see no hope of any substantial change in the condition of the historic churches, corrupted as they are by their compromises and defeated by their doubts." I referred to "the faithful remnant [that] needs to draw together. The weaknesses I have drawn attention to in the historic churches are self-indulgences one can afford in a period of stability, but not in an age of revolution." (By "the faithful remnant" I meant the Anglo-Catholics, evangelicals, and charismatics in the Church of England.)

I went on, "The choice before us is of a church armed with spiritual power, convinced of the faith, trusting in Jesus Christ and filled with the Holy Spirit, praying, fasting, forgiving, loving, dying; or of a church that compromises with the world, denies the faith, accepts the standards of the world, and worships at the shrine of the false god of humanism. Increasingly there will be a division between the two. For the truth's sake, the issues need to be seen and faced."

The lecture was printed and published (*Muster Christian Handbook,* 1979). It sold out five times, and innumerable magazines and newspapers reproduced it. A Catholic journal published it in full. Arthur Wallis, then a well-known leader in the so-called "restoration" movement among the house churches, published it in the magazine *Restoration*. I had more letters responding to this small book than to most of the other books I have written. Some whose judgment I greatly respect say it is the most important thing I have ever written. It obviously struck a chord with many people, who were getting tired of the ambivalent attitude of the church towards outrageous heresy. I was speaking for them. As for a drawing together of the faithful remnant, I was already taking steps to do something about this myself.

The Faith House Meetings

On August 10 of that year I went to see Dr. John Stott, then the leader of the Anglican evangelical world. I aired my concerns and he agreed personally to back the idea of bringing some of the remnant together. On September 18 I had a meeting with Dr. Eric Kemp, the Bishop of Chichester and soon to become my bishop. He was the acknowledged leader of the Anglo-Catholics in the Church of England. We met at his club in London. I remember the windows had been blown out the day before by a bomb planted by the Provisional IRA. He agreed to meet with Dr. John Stott and others to address the serious issues facing the Church of England at that time. Another person I approached was Canon David Watson, then at the height of his influence as an evangelical charismatic.[2]

The first meeting took place at Faith House, Westminster, in the offices of the Church Union, on February 14, 1980. It was the year that Lord Runcie was appointed Archbishop of Canterbury, so almost the first thing we did was to approach the Primate to ask if we could arrange a meeting at which to share with him the matters that concerned us. On September 19 that year he invited us to lunch at Lambeth Palace. We decided to raise two issues with him. The first was the book *The Myth of God Incarnate,* and the second was the question of homosexuality, which was then appearing on the horizon as a potentially divisive issue.

We were received with the outward grace but inward inscrutability that were to mark Lord Runcie's term as archbishop. One thing I remember about the discussions was the bland way in which he treated the homosexuality issue. He was never to come to terms with it throughout his time as archbishop, and he was to admit later that he had knowingly ordained practicing homosexuals. Another incident I remember was when John Stott told Lord Runcie that a Muslim publishing house in Egypt had quickly translated *The Myth of God Incarnate* into Arabic and that the book was now being widely distributed throughout the Middle East. I was looking straight at the face of the archbishop at that moment, and he was visibly shaken. Some things did get through his normally impenetrable outer shell.

The Faith House meetings were to continue for several years and, in hindsight, were a microcosm of what was happening in the Church of England. Eventually we produced the report *Towards a Renewed Church: A Joint Statement by Catholic, Charismatic and Evangelical Anglicans* (Grove Books, 1988). Among the signatories was George Carey, later to become Archbishop of Canterbury.

The statement made clear that all those who took part believed in the "givenness of truth." It went on, "Truth has been revealed by God within the community of his people. Although we value tradition, reason and experience for the important role they play in the interpretation of Scripture, yet the Church of England continues to attribute a normative authority to Scripture" (p. 2). The statement gave pre-eminence to "the Church's renewal in truth because everything else flows from it." It pointed out that the Spirit who brought renewal was also the Spirit of Truth: "Whenever he renews the Church, he renews it in the Truth. There is then a new humility and reverence before divine revelation, a new zeal to defend and proclaim it, and a new resolve to obey it" (p. 3).

The statement also dealt with moral issues. It was not ashamed to declare, "True marriage is monogamous, heterosexual and lifelong, and the only God-intended context for the enjoyment of sexual intercourse" (p. 4). It handled the issue of homosexuality. It welcomed "affectionate friendships between members of the same sex and of the opposite sex," but made clear that genital acts outside the marriage bond, whether heterosexual or homosexual, "are always deviations from the divine order, and, therefore, sinful" (p. 4).

(Since these meetings some evangelicals have retreated from this position. When homosexuals and lesbians celebrated their sexuality in the Anglican Southwark Cathedral in the autumn of 1996, the evangelical bishop of Guildford preached at the service and received a round of grateful applause from the gays present.)

The Faith House statement was published in 1988. I was able to give one of the first copies to Archbishop Robert Runcie at the National Evangelical Anglican Congress in Caistor that year. The bishop of Chichester used the booklet as study material for his diocese.

Dr. David Jenkins

The *Myth of God Incarnate* controversy was to be followed a few years later by the arrival in Durham of Dr. David Jenkins. By a strange coincidence, the day his appointment was announced my wife and I had been invited to dinner by Mr. Robin Catford. He was the Patronage Secretary, responsible with others for major church appointments. The Catfords lived just around the corner from us. As we started the meal Robin leaned over to me and asked, "What do you think of our new appointment to Durham?" My reply was non-committal, as I knew very little about Dr. Jenkins at the time.

His appointment plunged the Church of England into a serious crisis: a man who denied the faith was to become a bishop. At his consecration he would be called upon to declare his belief in the faith "revealed in the holy Scriptures and set forth in the catholic Creeds" (*Alternative Service Book,* 1980, p. 388). One of these Creeds, the Nicene, would be said in the service just before the bishop's declaration. It was quite clear from the beginning that Dr. Jenkins did not believe in the Nicene Creed as it has been taught and understood by the Church from the fourth century. Nor was he going to preach such a faith.

William Ledwich, now Father Athanasius Ledwich of the Greek Orthodox Church, organized a petition to try to get the consecration of the bishop in York Minster stopped. He has documented the story in his book, *The Durham Affair* (Stylite Publishing, 1985). The archbishop of York was urged to invite Dr. Jenkins to affirm his belief in the Creeds and, if he refused, to consider seriously whether it was right to go on with the consecration.

The archbishop refused to involve the bishop of Durham elect, writing that the affirmations in the service were enough, and the bishop would make them. If that were unacceptable to people, then they were calling into question his integrity and sincerity. The bishop was duly consecrated—and recited the Nicene Creed.

Throughout his time at Durham he was to pour scorn with great effectiveness on the faith of the Creed. In *The Lion, the Witch, and the Wardrobe,* C. S. Lewis says that in Narnia under the White Witch's curse it is "always winter and never Christmas."

It seemed that every Christmas the journalists made a meal of Dr. Jenkins's denials of the Incarnation, as if to make sure it was "never Christmas" for us. There is nothing journalists like more than an unbelieving bishop. Dr. Jenkins described the faith of people like myself as "worshipping a cultural idol" and said that belief in miracles is "immoral and demonic."

But the crux of the Durham affair was that *not a single bishop signed William Ledwich's petition.* Some disagreed with the bishop of Durham elect, but believed that he was as much entitled to his view as they were to theirs. The reality of this emerged from a poll in which diocesan bishops were asked about their views. Over thirty out of thirty-nine replied. Their responses were shattering. Ten did not believe in the historicity of the Virgin Birth. Nine did not believe in either the bodily or the spiritual Resurrection of Christ, thus expressing views even more radical than Dr. Jenkins's. To me the key question was, "Do you hold that it is necessary for Christians to believe that Christ is God?" Nineteen bishops did not consider it necessary.

It is no wonder that, because of this, many began to doubt if the Church of England is, as it claims to be in its formularies, "part of the one holy, catholic and apostolic Church." The thought began to cross my mind: "Can I stay in such a church?" Was it just coincidence that two nights after the bishop's consecration a freak flash of lightning struck York Minster and set it on fire? As the fire engines raced to York Minster, ringing their bells, so alarm bells began to ring loudly for us and for many others. Saint Augustine of Hippo once said, "If you believe what you like in the gospel and reject what you don't like, it is not the gospel you believe but yourself."

The Crockford's Preface

In the autumn of 1987, *Crockford's Clerical Directory* was published with its usual anonymous preface. This one was critical of the leadership of the Church of England, especially the bishops. There followed extreme pressure by the media to find out who had written it. Eventually authorship was traced to an Oxford theologian, Canon Gareth Bennett, who, when discovered, tragically took his own life.

I did not read the preface until 1993. I was too shocked by what had happened. When I did read it, I realized why some of the bishops and the media had reacted in the way they did. It was not primarily because of Gareth Bennett's critique of the archbishop of Canterbury. He knew the archbishop well, and they were old friends. The thing that upset the "establishment" most was his analysis of the fault lines running through the Church of England, which were often mirrored in the archbishop of Canterbury, who consistently "nailed his colours to the fence," to quote the phrase used by Canon Bennett in the preface. Canon Bennett was dotting too many "i"s and crossing too many "t"s for comfort.

William Oddie has written a book called *The Crockford's File,* which documents this sad affair (Hamish Hamilton, 1989). He sums up these happenings thus: "It is a portrait of a Church whose representative leaders have turned against Scripture and Tradition as their chief guides, and now rely principally on the ephemeral wisdom of the passing age." In other words, their thinking is governed by the secular norms of pluralism, relativism, and subjectivism.

"Beliefless Christianity"

Just around the corner from where we live is a village called Staplefield. The vicar of the church there, a man called Anthony Freeman, wrote in 1993 a book called *God in Us* (SCM, 1993), in which he made it plain that he no longer believed in the Incarnation, the Resurrection, or life after death. He wanted to be free to stay on as a priest and preach a "new, bracing, beliefless Christianity." This was going full circle; here was a priest in office who did not believe in anything that we might call Christian. Yet he continued to preach and administer the sacraments, regarding these as "good for people." How can it be that a church that claims to be Christian can sustain in office someone who by no stretch of the imagination can be called Christian in his beliefs? In this case his bishop (Dr. Eric Kemp) did something about it. He asked Freeman to consider his position for a year and then, since he had not changed his views, removed his license.

Another priest, the Rev. Hugh Dawes, wrote a book even more radical than Freeman's. It came out the year before Freeman's and was called *Freeing the Faith,* with the subtitle *A Credible Christianity for Today* (SPCK, 1992). There are many other priests in the Church of England whose thinking is the same. A letter signed by this group and bearing sixty-five signatures, including that of a former dean of St. Paul's, was published in the *Independent* newspaper on July 23, 1994. They protested against Bishop Eric Kemp's decision to dismiss the Rev. Anthony Freeman and called it a "day of sorrow." They criticized the bishop's action as "reversing a long Church of England tradition that tolerates and values a wide range of views." But who is to decide the extent of that range? Does it have boundaries? Here we see religious pluralism again.

It seems clear now from Humphrey Carpenter's biography of Lord Runcie (Hodder & Stoughton, 1996) that the Primate also had very little clear faith in anything. He was helped, apparently, by a Cambridge theologian who taught him he could be "unbelieving, incredulous and still a good Anglo-Catholic."[3] Later Kierkegaard showed him, as he put it, "a way in which I could hold together a fundamental scepticism with religious devotion."

It is not surprising, therefore, that Lord Runcie chose an

agnostic to write his biography. Lord Runcie said frivolously that he hoped the biographer might be converted. One has to ask—to what? In her review of the biography, Minette Marrin wrote, "If any of this tends towards anybody's 'conversion' the word has been drained of all meaning. Indeed my own brief encounters with Anglican theology have convinced me that its main impetus is to construct a language meaningless enough for the clergy to disguise their own lack of faith from themselves" (*Sunday Telegraph,* Nov. 22, 1996). Or, as it was explained to James Hacker in the TV series, "Yes, Prime Minister," "You cannot appoint a bishop who does not believe in God, so you call him a modernist."

In May, 1996, the Prince of Wales announced that he intended to be "Defender of Faith" rather than "Defender of *the* Faith" when he became king. Janet Daley wrote at the time in the *Daily Telegraph* (May 10, 1996), "If the idea of belief is all that matters, no religious belief can be seen as false. And if no religion is false, then none is true. By presenting all faiths as equally valid, they all become equally spurious."

This is the kind of thing the Anglican Church has done within the parameters of the Christian Faith. The liberties the Anglican Reformers demanded (for themselves, not for Roman Catholics or Dissenters), and the consensus sought in the Elizabethan Settlement, made it inevitable that this situation would arise. No wonder many are looking wistfully in the direction of the Orthodox and Roman Catholic churches. These churches consider their main role as passing on faithfully the Truth that has come down to them from Christ through the Apostles and defending that faith against all those who would tamper with it. It is not surprising, therefore, that a growing number see this as the right way forward. They want to find a way of escaping the flood of liberalism that is engulfing not only the Anglican but all Protestant churches.

The Last Straw

The last straw for us was the decision of the General Synod to ordain women to the priesthood. It seemed that here was a church making decisions contrary, in the first place, to the example of Christ, who chose only men to be his Apostles; in the second, to the plain teaching of the Scriptures, which see men having headship over women in the Church and in the family; in the third, to the unanimous opinion of the Church Fathers, and the consensus of the Church that the priest is an icon of Christ, as the Orthodox say, and so must be male.

Here one could discern the fault lines of Anglicanism. In its decision can be seen its proneness to trendiness rather than truth. It was ignoring Catholic Christendom, of which the Church of England claims to be a part. We see also the concern of its bishops for unity at the expense of truth, without which unity has no meaning. This unity has been called by Dr. Graham Leonard "the club mentality" that subjects "the demands of unity based on truth to the needs of not rocking the boat" (*New Directions,* June 1993, p. 16).

It would be perfectly proper for someone, in the light of this analysis of the flaws in Anglicanism, to ask the questions, "Why didn't you leave earlier?" or, "Why wait for the decision to ordain women to the priesthood? Surely denying the Resurrection is considerably more important than ordaining women?" There is no easy answer to these legitimate questions. It is easier to provide reasons for leaving than reasons for *not* doing so.

The spread of liberalism in the Anglican and other Protestant churches has been alarming. Yet it has to be said that the views of the former Bishop of Durham, Dr. David Jenkins, to give an example, were his personal ones, and not the official position of the Church of England. I had grown up to glory in the comprehensiveness of this church. I had realized that you can't have it both ways. If it was tolerant enough to accept evangelical positions, why not liberal? Since the Church of England officially accepts the Nicene Creed, it seemed possible to remain a member in spite of those liberals who denied parts of it. Truth was worth fighting for within this church, and there was more than a chance that these departures from the truth could be corrected.

However, when the decision was taken to ordain women to the priesthood, it was passed by the General Synod and became immediately the doctrine, and soon after, the practice of the whole Anglican Church. No one was bound to follow Dr. Jenkins, but the whole church was affected by the decision to ordain women to the priesthood. In this case there was no way the decision could be reversed in the foreseeable future.

The Anglican Middle Way

John Henry Newman, in his Anglican days, pinned his hopes for the future on what he called "the Anglican Via Media" or the middle way. Many of the "Tracts for the Times" which he published reflected this effort at justifying Catholic practices in the Church of England. They were attempts to drive a way between the Scylla and Charybdis of Roman Catholicism and Protestantism, although their arguments were sometimes strained. The Tractarians, as they were called, began their Oxford Movement as distinctly anti-Roman Catholic, but, as Stephen Thomas has written of Newman, "Under the confident surface of his Tractarian rhetoric unresolved problems were lurking."[4]

The crisis for Newman came in 1839. He spent much of that summer studying the Christological controversies of the first half of the fifth century, which centered initially on Saint Cyril, the Archbishop of Alexandria, and Nestorius, the Archbishop of Constantinople from 429 to 431. This dispute led ultimately to schism, beginning after the Council of Ephesus

(431). The Oriental Orthodox separated from the Eastern Orthodox churches. The Oriental Orthodox include the Egyptian Coptic Church, the Ethiopian Coptic Church, the Syrian Jacobite Church, and the Armenian Orthodox Church. (The Armenians were not represented at Chalcedon because of their involvement in a serious war.)

During the summer Newman wrote a long paper on this subject which was never published, but it seems that this was the turning-point for him. Later he wrote: "Now here, in the middle of the fifth century, I found, as it seemed to me Christendom of the sixteenth and nineteenth centuries reflected. I saw my face in that mirror, *and l was a Monophysite.* The Church of the 'Via Media' was in the position of the Oriental Communion, Rome was where she now is; and the Protestants were the Eutychians."[5] In his *Apologia* Newman writes of this period of his life, "For the first time a doubt came upon me of the tenableness of Anglicanism."[6]

Throughout his life Newman was an obsessive heresy hunter, although his enthusiasm cooled once he was safe in the Roman fold. But why did he see himself as a Monophysite?[7] He agreed with the Ecumenical Councils of Ephesus (431) and Chalcedon (451), which defined the two natures of Christ. The key is to be found in his *Apologia.* There Newman makes it clear that it was not the Christological doctrine to which he was referring. Rather he had in mind the dangers of a moderate position, of a Via Media, in dogmatic controversies. *It was in the way the heretics of this period did their theology that Newman saw the connection with Anglicanism.*

There were some in this period who had a solid and disciplined way of thinking through complex theological issues, such as the Cappadocian Fathers,[8] Saint Cyril of Alexandria, and Saint Athanasius, whereas heretics such as Eutyches and Nestorius were superficial and inconsistent. Georges Florovsky, a twentieth-century Orthodox theologian, wrote about "the frivolousness of Monophysite thought and the vagueness of its theological vision."[9]

The basis of heresy is compromise. The Greek root of "heretic" means "one who chooses." A heretic chooses, or is selective in, what he believes, what he embraces and what he discards. A key figure at this time was Theodoret (393–458), the Bishop of Cyrrhus and a native of Antioch. He wrote something he called *Eranistes.*[10] The word means "one who makes a garment from discarded rags." That was how he saw the heresies of his day. Few heresies are novel. Most modern ones are as Theodoret described them, "old rags."

Heretics drive their arguments down the middle of the road; that is what Newman suddenly discovered. It was where Newman saw Anglicanism, and as a result his own Via Media arguments in defense of his Church shattered into pieces. This point has been well made by Martin Svaglic, who writes, "It is not the doctrines themselves which are significant for Newman's point of view, but rather *the mode in which a solution was reached"* (italics mine).[11] From 1839 onwards, Newman was on his way to Rome.

In a flash Newman had come to see that the Via Media was the highway of heretics. It was a way of fudging issues for the sake of peace and unity. It could lead only to compromise and confusion, not to an understanding of the truth. The Church Fathers were not Via Media people, like modern Anglicans. In the Byzantine Church the duty of the bishops, especially when they attended the Ecumenical Councils, was, as John McGuckin writes, "to 'recognise' by comparison with past precedent, the faith of the Church and, having recognised it, acclaim it in the Spirit."[12] It was essentially to follow the way of the Apostles, who had been inspired by the Holy Spirit, rather than to follow the fashions of the moment. Theirs was an implicit calling to stand as bishops in the apostolic succession. McGuckin goes on:

> It was not expected, therefore, that senior hierarchs should have to agonise about what the faith was, or search out its meaning; given they had lived by it for years and were holding the ecclesiastical office as teachers of the faith. . . . In short, an open and neutral enquiry over doctrine that was designed to achieve an internationally acceptable compromise was never in the minds or expectations of any of those attending the Council of Ephesus, except perhaps Nestorius. This concept of the definition of Christianity by progressive compromise was, and still is, alien to the Orthodox and Catholic Communions.

There are modern approaches to this. We are used to the demands of democratic processes in politics. There is a premium on gentlemanly and ladylike conduct and fair play. A variety of opinions and intellectual arguments is encouraged. This marks present-day attitudes to truth, with the inevitable compromises that follow. However, such ways were alien to the Church Fathers. They still are alien today to the Orthodox Church's understanding of the truth as found in the Scriptures and the rest of Holy Tradition.

Certainly the new doctrines of the Church of England were objectionable to us, but the way that decisions were arrived at was wholly unacceptable. For some people Nestorius was a gentleman and Saint Cyril a cad. But in the end it was the heretical views of the one that were rejected and the orthodox stand of the other that was supported.

One of the first Anglicans to move to the Roman Catholic Church after the decision to ordain women to the priesthood was Sheridan Gilley, whom I have already mentioned. He wrote in *The Times* (Nov. 11, 1993) of the intellectual and spiritual powerlessness of the Church of England to resist the wisdom of this passing world. He went on to say that this partly explains "why so many of the Church's greatest saints and prophets either, like Wesley, pass their lives in the disgrace of internal exile within her or are compelled to leave her, like Newman." The Prophet Isaiah challenged the people of his day with the words, "Woe to those who call evil good, and good evil;/Who put darkness for light, and light for darkness;/Who put bitter for sweet, and sweet for bitter!" (Is. 5:20). The churches have been called to the unpopular task of defending landmarks, not moving them.

Mary Poppins, in the book and movie of that name, floats down from space as a kind of "messianic" figure. At the end of the movie, the wind changes direction and she floats off again in the direction of St. Pancras station. Before she goes she packs her things in front of the children, who are desolate. They plead with her to stay. She replies, "Practically perfect people never permit sentiment to muddle their thinking." It's a message we all should heed. Newman once wrote, "Religion as a mere sentiment is to me a dream and a mockery."[13] The Church Fathers were not perfect or even practically perfect, and certainly this writer is not. However, as we floated off in the direction of Antioch and said our good-byes to our Anglican friends, we refused to allow sentiment to muddle our thinking.

1 Ed. John Hick, SCM, 1977.

2 The joint signatories were: Dr. Christina Baxter, Rt. Rev. George Carey, Mr. Maurice Chandler, CBE, Canon Christopher Colvin, Mrs. Sue Flockton, Rev. Peter Geldard, Rev. David Gillett, Canon John Gunstone, Rt. Rev. Peter Hall, Canon Michael Harper, Rt. Rev. Eric Kemp, Canon Peter Peterken and Rev. John Stott. Others who took part: Rev. Roger Beckwith, Mrs. Jill Dann, Mr. Raymond Johnston,

the Rt. Rev. Richard Rutt and Canon David Watson.

3 J. S. Bezzant, quoted in the biography, pp. 52 and 88.

4 *Newman and Heresy: The Anglican Years,* CUP, 1991, p. 171.

5 *Apologia Pro Vita Sua,* p. 114. Eutyches was a monk in Constantinople whose views were condemned by the Church in 448 and again at the Council of Chalcedon in 451. He had a reputation for frequently shifting his ground, especially under pressure. He insisted on the one nature of the incarnate Word and appeared to deny the full humanity of Christ.

6 Ibid.

7 The term "Monophysite" needs to be explained. It means "of one nature." In the controversies concerning the natures of Christ in the fifth century, it was unfortunate that the two sides misunderstood each other from time to time and were even guilty of accusing the other side of beliefs it never held. The so-called Monophysites never believed that Christ only had one nature (the divine), but always upheld his full and true humanity. The confusion was often between "person" and "nature." The Orthodox Church has always believed that Christ was one person and that he had two natures.

8 St. Basil the Great, Bishop of Caesarea (c. 330–79), St. Gregory of Nyssa (c. 330–c. 395), the younger brother of St. Basil, and St. Gregory of Nazianzus (329–89), called "the Theologian." They were all Cappadocians by birth and, together with St. Athanasius, were the chief influence in the overthrow of Arianism.

9 *Collected Works,* Vol. 8, Büchervertriebsanstalt, 1987, p. 292.

10 Described by Henry Chadwick, *The Early Church,* Penguin, 1967, p. 201.

11 Quoted by Stephen Thomas (p. 205) from the introduction to the edition of *Apologia Pro Vita Sua* published by the Clarendon Press in 1967.

12 *St. Cyril of Alexandria: The Christological Controversy, its History, Theology and Texts,* Brill, 1994, pp. 70–71.

13 He also said, "From the age of fifteen [his evangelical conversion], dogma has been the fundamental principle of my religion: I know no other religion, I cannot enter into the idea of any other sort of religion." *History of My Religious Opinions from 1839 to 1841.*

4

Discovering Orthodoxy

. . . Half to forget the wandering and the pain
Half to remember days that have gone by
And dream and dream that I am Home again.
James Elroy Flecker

Jesus said that His Kingdom was like treasure hidden in a field or like a merchant looking for valuable pearls. To find the treasure, and to buy the pearls, there needs to be a great deal of effort and not a little sacrifice. Orthodoxy is like that. You have to work hard to find and secure it, and be most determined also. There is something essentially hidden and mysterious about Orthodoxy that does not fit easily into the culture of Western consumerism and its marketing thrust; it runs counter to modern demands for openness and the "sales pitch" of our approach, particularly in the Protestant world, to "mission." Sometimes it seems as if the Orthodox are not too concerned whether people become Orthodox or not, yet I have found this to be one of the most appealing things about the Orthodox Church: it doesn't go out of its way to convert you.[1] Its prime concern in practice is the realm of worship.

We need to view this attitude against the background of the history of Orthodoxy in Western Europe. There are some similarities here with the Jews. Both Orthodox people and Jews came to Western Europe from the East, often as refugees. They came to societies that were culturally different from, even alien to, their own. So they have tended to develop an enclosed mentality. They have had to struggle against the temptation and pressure to lose their identity and become absorbed into the society and culture of the West. This has been the main reason why there has been a lack of a sense of mission in the Orthodox Church in the West. They have seen their role as preservative rather than evangelistic. Both Orthodox people and Jews have also tended to look to the East for their roots and to North America for their support. But in one respect British Orthodoxy is different. The original roots of Christianity in Britain are more Eastern than Western, and the sources of the Celtic Church were more Byzantine than Roman. This is due largely to the geography of the British Isles. At the time of Christ's life on earth they were attracting trade from the eastern Mediterranean, unlike most of the rest of Europe.

When the journey to Orthodoxy began, we found barriers in the way. At the start of our pilgrimage a few of us had an appointment with a leading Orthodox bishop. He spent the first ten minutes telling us how wonderful he thought the Church of England was. He expressed surprise that we should want to become Orthodox. When my wife and I visited India just before our reception into the Orthodox Church, we had an appointment with the Catholicos of the Orthodox Syrian Church in India, Baselius Marthoma Mathews I. The conversation went much the same way. He spent the first part of our time together trying to put us off becoming Orthodox. "Don't do that without a great deal of prayer," he pleaded with us.

The Orthodox didn't seem keen to talk. Then a friend gave me a key which in the end opened many Orthodox doors. "When you contact the Orthodox, don't ask to go and talk theology with them," he said. "Say to them, may I come and pray with you?" For some this may seem like a false kind of piety. Yet it pointed the way for me as nothing else had done. Timothy (Bishop Kallistos) Ware, in his book, *The Orthodox Church,* writes: "Those who wish to know about Orthodoxy should not so much read books as . . . attend the Liturgy" (p. 266).

He goes on to quote the words of Christ to Andrew: "Come and see" (John 1:39). You need to come and see Orthodoxy as well as read about it.

My earliest contact with Orthodoxy was entirely surprising and unsought. One would not expect to find it in a Pentecostal university! I was on a visit to Oral Roberts University in Tulsa, Oklahoma, during the 1970s. I stayed with Dr. Bob Stamps, who was then the Methodist chaplain. I remember he had just written a song, and he sat at the piano and sang it to me. It was "God and Man at Table Are Sat Down," and I introduced it in Britain when I got back. It proved popular, though I did not realize its strong Orthodox overtones at the time.[2] The university, believe it or not, was experiencing an Orthodox revival, with a Friday Vespers service, a processional crucifix, and incense. Sadly, not much of it rubbed off on me.

In 1989 an international group of church leaders began to plan a large conference, which was to be held in Brighton, England, in 1991. I was appointed the chairman. One of my duties was to contact the Orthodox with a view to their being invited as delegates. (We were not that hopeful, so we allocated fifty places out of a total of over three thousand delegates. In the event only twelve came.) But to fulfill this undertaking some of us went on a short tour of the Middle East, and visited Finland.

The trip to Finland was a milestone on the journey. Three of us went there in January, 1990, in the middle of a particularly cold winter. It was -25°C when we got on the sleeper train in Helsinki to travel to a remote corner of the Finnish tundra, the monastery of New Valamo, at Heinävesi.

Old Valamo (or Valaam) is a famous monastery in Russia founded in the twelfth century, which was attended regularly by Tsar Nicholas II and his family. In fact, the furniture of the royal suite is now in the new monastery. There we saw the simple life of the monks of this famous center of spiritual life to which many Finns go, though they normally choose more clement weather.

That Sunday I attended one of my first Orthodox Divine Liturgies. I should explain that the Orthodox use the word "liturgy" to describe what others call the service of the Eucharist or the Holy Communion. My first thought was, "How relaxed." The service ran through most of the morning, and people came and went; no one seemed bothered. We went out for a cup of coffee halfway through and didn't feel the least bit guilty.[3] The Liturgy, which has since come to have the primary place in my life, was the Divine Liturgy of Saint John Chrysostom. It was said and sung in Finnish.

It was one of those moments when an event becomes etched indelibly in one's mind and heart. I still recall it as if it were yesterday. I remember David Goodenough, a friend who was with us and was suffering from ME, asking a member of the congregation if they prayed for the sick. He was directed without embarrassment to an icon where healings were known to take place. (Who said the Orthodox Church isn't charismatic?)

My other memories are of an old man who stood throughout the service (there were no pews in the chapel) and of the expression on his face. It was not the glow of a charismatic or the boredom of some Western worshippers. I was reminded of the faces of old Russian women, their expression of eternal faithfulness. One might be tempted to call it stoical disregard for the circumstances or the fashions of the times. Yet there was nothing stoical about this man. For me he epitomized solid faithfulness, the quality that has made Orthodox laity stalwart defenders of the Faith down the centuries.

The Liturgy was being served by a young Finnish Orthodox bishop. I will never forget his kindness and thoughtfulness. He greeted us and invited us to sit with him for the early part of the service, so that he could explain it all to us. He welcomed us to share in the so-called *antidoron* and to reverence the cross at the end of the Liturgy. The *antidoron* is unconsecrated but blessed bread, offered as a token of brotherly love to all Orthodox in the congregation, but also to guests who are not Orthodox. It is also a symbol of taking the gospel to the whole world.

After everyone had gone, Bishop Ambrosius invited us to the sauna to carry on our discussions. How Finnish! In that country almost everything that is important is done in the sauna, and this was no exception. So one of the most significant things I learned was how culturally adjustable Orthodoxy can be. I did not feel then, and never have since, that the Eastern Liturgy is culturally foreign to an Englishman. It is no more strange to me than the Bible is. Here was Orthodoxy fitting like a glove into Finnish culture. One may be tempted to think of Orthodoxy as intended for hot eastern climates; here we had been worshipping God in a chapel where the outside temperature was -25°C, and doing it in Finnish, not Greek or Slavonic. It is true the bishop had a beard (I have met some who haven't), but he was thoroughly Finnish. It helped me see that the Orthodox Church fits all cultures, climates, and situations—even saunas.

One has to face the fact that in Western Europe there is a great deal of ignorance about Orthodoxy. When I was about to join the Orthodox Church I wrote to my sisters to tell them what was going to happen. I had roughly the same response from two of them. "Thank God you are not going to become a Catholic. *What is the Orthodox Church?*" This says a lot about the ingrained suspicion and prejudice that persists in Britain against Catholicism. But it also reveals starkly that most people in Britain know little or nothing about the Orthodox Church.

I have to confess that for many years I was as ignorant as anyone else. Yet two factors kept me asking the question, "What is this Church?" In the first place, I had a deep interest in, and concern for, the Church itself, not as an institution but as it really is, the "Body of Christ." And second, there was in me an underlying passion for Christian unity and a sense of corporate guilt that the churches were so divided and that progress towards unity seemed so slow. The Orthodox Church could not be left out of that equation.[4]

An early indication of some of the seed thoughts that were in my mind was the book I wrote in 1979 called *This is the Day* (Hodder & Stoughton; it was published in the United States with the title *The Three Sisters*). In the book I explored the theme that had already been opened up by people like Dr. Lesslie Newbigin, in his book *The Household of God* (SCM, 1953), and Dr. Henry Pitt Van Dusen in an article in *Time* magazine called "The Third Force." I shall be referring to the former in more detail in chapter 13. These writers re-examined the Church, normally seen as having two main polarities, Catholic and Protestant, with a third element, the Pentecostal.

In my book readers were introduced to the three "sisters" in the family of the Church, whom I called Evangeline, Charisma, and Roma. Here I was following the same pattern as the other writers. But I mentioned another member of the family. I wrote:

> I know there is at least one more sister that I have never really met. I have sometimes seen her in the distance. I understand her name is Orthodoxa. *Somehow the rest of the family seems incomplete without her.* I have to confess I have neither avoided her nor made strenuous efforts to meet her and get to know her. Our paths have very seldom crossed . . . but this book is sadly incomplete without her. *Maybe the next big movement of the Holy Spirit will be the enrichment of our family life with the*

inclusion in close friendship of Orthodoxa—and this sister's own enrichment also in sharing openly with her other sisters.

If I were writing that book now, I would not describe Orthodoxa as a fourth, rather neglected, sister. Rather, I would say that she is the Mother Church, and the three sisters Evangeline, Charisma, and Roma all her more or less wayward daughters. Each daughter has some of the characteristics of the mother, but only the mother contains the fullness of what Christ intended His Church to be.

But at that early stage of my journey, I recognized only that there was something present in Orthodoxy that I had not found elsewhere. I was still almost a complete stranger to its life and teaching.

Having said all this, there is at least one advantage to ignorance of Orthodoxy: most people don't know enough about us to be prejudiced against us. No Orthodox Armada set sail to bring Britain under its heel. No Orthodox blood has been shed in Britain for the last thousand years to defend the faith of our Church. Mostly people have vague notions about bearded, cassocked priests, icons, incense, long services, and an absence of pews. Obviously we have a lot to explain about our Orthodox Church, the second largest in the world. (On a recent visit to the USA I brought back an Orthodox bumper sticker that says, "Preaching the gospel since AD 33"—and so we have been!)

Orthodoxy, for me, is like one of those old metal chests, covered with the dust of centuries. But when you pry it open—and how hard it is to do that—you find the chest full of jewels. So many people never see the riches; they see only the outward dust. When I was a student at Cambridge, I studied theology for three years. I do not remember ever being recommended any Orthodox books to read, let alone having one as a set book in the syllabus. I did not even know the name of a single theologian from this tradition, apart from Nicholas Zernov. The only Orthodox leader I had ever heard of was Metropolitan Anthony of Sourozh.

Now I have discovered some of the truly great writers and theologians of this century, men like Georges Florovsky, Vladimir Lossky, Alexander Schmemann, John Meyendorff, and many others. What a lot I had missed! These men write with a prophetic instinct, a deep commitment to the Orthodox Faith, and a humble respect for the truth. There are few books I read more than once, and even fewer more than twice. But Bishop Kallistos Ware's book *The Orthodox Church* (Penguin Books, 1963, rev. ed. 1993) I have read three times, buying each updated edition as it has been published. At an early stage in my pilgrimage I went to Oxford to meet the author. He received me with great kindness and gentleness.

It was while on a visit to Zaïre that I had a brief encounter with the Oriental Orthodox Church that I will always cherish. I was in a party representing the World Council of Churches, and we were the guests of the Kimbanguist Church, which is one of the largest of the African Independent churches. The church, a member of the World Council of Churches, was founded by a man called Simon Kimbangu in the 1920s and had suffered a great deal of persecution from the Belgian colonial rulers. Simon Kimbangu himself spent most of his life in prison.

We were waiting for dinner one evening and, as usual, were having a heated discussion. The party included Dr. Walter Hollenweger, who was then Professor of Mission at Birmingham University in England, and Bishop Markos of the Egyptian Coptic Church, who was living in Nairobi. The subject of our discussion was the teaching of the Kimbanguist Church on the Trinity. It seemed to us that it was, at that time, unitarian.

Now, I have known Walter for a long time, and he loves to play the part of *agent provocateur*. This time he got more than he bargained for. "Of course," he said in as casual a tone of voice as he could muster, "some of the Church Fathers were unitarian." At that the Egyptian Coptic bishop got to his feet and strode quickly over to Walter. I thought for a moment he was going to hit him. There followed a tirade in defense of the Church Fathers such as I had never heard before. Here was passion, and no holds barred. I flagged in my memory this note: "The Orthodox Church doesn't mess around with truth. They love the truth so much they'll defend it at the drop of a hat."

In the last few years we have met many Orthodox people; we have been shown great kindness—although, it has to be added, a few have made life difficult for us. I cannot help being reminded of the parable of the prodigal son, a story that the Orthodox Church focuses on as it approaches Great Lent. Those of us in Britain who became Orthodox through the Antiochian Patriarchate were welcomed home with open arms, but there were a few older brothers around who were indignant that we were being made such a fuss of. They also criticized our table manners. For myself, I don't think the father of the prodigal worried too much whether his son used a spoon or a fork to eat his dinner or wiped his fingers on his shirt or the tablecloth. It was just good to have his son home. In time the manners would be corrected. Our Orthodox manners were far from perfect. We got some things wrong, and we had a great deal to learn. Yet home is a far better place to learn it in than the far country.

1 It has to be said that sometimes this is taken too far by the Orthodox; there are a growing number of people who genuinely want to become Orthodox and, without resorting to crude promotion, their desires should be taken seriously. It is possible for this to be done in a humble

spirit and without giving offense.

2 The first two verses are:

O welcome, all ye noble saints of old
As now before your very eyes unfold
The wonders all so long ago foretold:
God and man at table are sat down.
Elders, martyrs, all are falling down,
Prophets, patriarchs are gathering round.
What angels longed to see now man has found.
God and man at table are sat down.

It would hardly pass the politically correct standards of today. Wayward sons are mentioned, but the only women alluded to specifically are "harlots." When it came out this aspect was completely unnoticed. Fashions have changed.

3 Now that I am Orthodox, I would feel guilty for this; it is the Orthodox practice to observe a complete fast from awakening until partaking of Holy Communion.

4 The Orthodox Church in Britain is the fourth largest, after the Roman Catholic, the Anglican, and the Methodist. The 1995 Marc Europe figures (published in the UK Christian Handbook) show that there are 287,510 Orthodox, of which the Greek Orthodox (Ecumenical Patriarchate) number 270,000. The Orthodox Church, unlike most others, is growing in Britain.

5

The Parting of Friends

Anglicanism is not a system of religion nor a body of truth, but a feeling, a tradition, its roots intertwined with associations of natural history and of family life; you do not learn it, you grow into it; you do not forget it, you grow out of it.

Monsignor Ronald Knox

When John Henry Newman parted company with the Church of England, he chose as the subject of his final sermon "the parting of friends." One of the prices, I thought, of leaving the church of my birth would be the loss of many friends. I dreaded the painful and resentful letters I might receive. I expected that some would accuse me of betraying the church I had been a member of for such a long time. At some of the worst moments, I felt I was a traitor and was ashamed of what I was about to do.

In the event, nothing like this happened. I received no adverse press and no hate mail. Many of my Anglican friends wrote to me, and I treasure their letters. They breathed only kindness and love. It was for us, as for Newman, a "parting of friends."

Yet we must not minimize the depth or the extent of the break. We can never again have Holy Communion in the Church of England, and as an Orthodox priest I can never give the holy gifts to any Anglicans—that is, until communion is restored, and the hope of that happening in my lifetime is remote. For, if anything, our two churches are drifting further and further apart. If one has a poor view of the Eucharist, and it does not have absolute priority in one's life as the most important thing we do, then it may not seem to matter too much if we don't share in it together. However, once it has the place that the Orthodox give to it, which Jeanne and I have fully embraced, then to be separated from other Christians at that most holy moment is extremely painful.

On November 11, 1992, an event took place which will be for ever etched on my mind. On the eleventh day of the eleventh month the General Synod of the Church of England decided by a two-thirds majority to ordain women to the priesthood. At the time I was suffering from shingles, but the pain caused by this event was a great deal worse and was to last for over two years. The memory of those years is still tender. The scenes outside Church House, Westminster, that November evening were dramatic: on the one hand, men and women danced for joy and, on the other, people like ourselves were in the deepest despair. It felt as if a doctor had told me that I had some terminal disease and had only a short time to live.

Some years ago Elisabeth Kübler-Ross wrote a book that became a bestseller called *On Death and Dying* (Macmillan, 1969). It attempted to analyze the stages that many people go through after they have been told that their illness is terminal. I found myself going through the same experience when I knew that my remaining time in the Church of England would be short.

Denial and Isolation

The first stage is *denial and isolation.* One says to oneself, "This is not true. It hasn't really happened." I remember waking up in the morning and telling myself, "It was a nightmare I had." Then the truth dawned that it wasn't a fantasy after all—it really was happening, I was "dying." Most patients doubt the diagnosis, question the X-ray, or believe in some magic cure. So

I found myself hoping against hope that our bishops would find some miraculous way out of the problem that would satisfy my conscience. When they met in Manchester the January after the vote, I hoped some compromise might be found. Perhaps the law of the land, Parliament, or even the Queen herself would come to the rescue and preserve the *status quo*. No such luck. It didn't happen.

Anger

The second stage is *anger*. And angry I certainly was, on and off, for quite a while. I expressed my anger in quite extraordinary and often uncharacteristic behavior. A lot of stuff I wrote never got published (fortunately). I fulminated against the system. I felt let down and betrayed. "This is how they treat someone who has worked for them for nearly forty years," I said to myself. Since I was so near to retirement, why couldn't it have happened a few years later? Like John Knox, I was angry with that "monstrous regiment of women" and, like him, I wanted to give a shrill blast on my trumpet.

I wrote steamy letters to bishops and others I thought might reverse this decision. (The action was futile, but it helped me work through my anger.) I had kind and courteous replies from them. Some of the bishops conducted a brilliant public relations operation. I remember that when I wrote to the Archbishop of York, Dr. Habgood, I had a reply by return of post. He had obviously read my letter carefully and sympathized with the position I was in.

Fortunately for me and everyone else, especially my wife and our associates, this phase was comparatively short. Paul, in his letter to the Ephesians, admits the need for anger, but in strictly limited doses. " 'Be angry, and do not sin,' " he writes. "Do not let the sun go down on your wrath, nor give place to the devil" (Eph. 4:26, 27). Also James gave us wise advice when he wrote, "The wrath of man does not produce the righteousness of God" (James 1:20). The fire soon subsided and burned itself out.

Bargaining

The third stage is bargaining, and I did plenty of that. I entered a period of scheming, of trying to find a way out which would satisfy my conscience and keep me in the Anglican Church. The idea emerged of attaching myself to an overseas diocese where women were not accepted as priests. I even contacted one bishop with a view to this. The thought crossed my mind of becoming an exile and living overseas. That made me feel rather virtuous.

Further encouragement to the bargaining stage was given when I read Sheldon Vanauken's book *Under the Mercy* (Hodder & Stoughton, 1985). Vanauken was converted through C.S. Lewis, and through his influence became a Roman Catholic. Sheldon asked an interesting question: How was it that C.S. Lewis, who influenced so many people to become Roman Catholics, never became one himself? One possible explanation is that Lewis was brought up in Ulster and had acquired a deep prejudice against Catholicism that he never completely threw off. For a man with such a clear and reasoning mind, this was some prejudice. So the thought occurred to me (I was bargaining again) that I could spend the rest of my life helping people to become Orthodox while remaining a noncollaborating Anglican myself.

Depression

The fourth stage of the process is *depression.* This was the lot of thousands of Anglicans following the decision of the General Synod—sadly, one has to add that it still is. To varying degrees we all went through "the dark night of the soul." In my case it was not helped by the fact that some of the Orthodox were not putting out the welcome mat. Everything at this time seemed bleak and miserable. I felt like an involuntary exile. It was like the experience of Abraham described in the Epistle to the Hebrews: "Here we have no continuing city" (Heb. 13:14).

At times there was an overwhelming sense that the whole of my life had been a waste of time and that everything had been useless. I felt like a gambling man who has put his shirt on the wrong horse and lost everything. At times my faith wavered. Why had God allowed this to happen? Those were dark days.

Acceptance

Yet the despair was a thousand times worthwhile, because finally we arrived at stage five—*acceptance.* Yes, peace did return. A sense of being born "for such a time as this" was recovered. The whole experience, and our reaction to it, assumed a better sense of proportion. The reconstruction of our shattered lives began. Anglican death was going to be swallowed up by Orthodox resurrection.

But what about the Church of England? After all, I had been a member of it for sixty-four years. Was that not "home"? I had a real struggle over this for a long time. It seemed to me that I was guilty of ingratitude for all that the Anglican Church had given me and done for me. That I could even contemplate leaving such a Church and moving to another, let alone do it, seemed to indicate a lack of appreciation. How could I explain such a thing?

Then one day I found a way of adjusting my thinking about this dilemma. I saw the Church of England as my *foster mother.* She had looked after me with great devotion until I found my real mother. Now I had "come home" to where I was always meant to be, where my real mother was, the place God had always intended and prepared for me. But could I ever forget my foster mother? No way! She had in a sense prepared me for this great homecoming. She must be held in honor, for she did the very best she could for me. I will always love her and respect her. There is in much of Anglicanism, with all its faults, a great kindness. This has been celebrated by the words of the poet John Dryden:

> See how his church, adorned with every grace
> With open arms, a kind forgiving face . . .

We were leaving behind a company that has included great saints and scholars, men and women who have been at the center of the development of something essentially British, of which we are proud. We were joining a Church that is practically unknown in Britain, with many uncertainties about the future.

We felt we were retracing our steps to a degree, although covering totally different territory. We remembered how we left All Souls Church, Langham Place, in 1964 to launch out in a new ministry, also with a most uncertain future. At that time we felt like Abraham leaving Ur of the Chaldees. It was said, "He went out, not knowing where he was going." He had to make his home in the promised land "by faith" (Heb. 11:8, 9). Now we were doing it again, with the benefit of thirty more years of experience and the testing of faith.

During this time we had a card from an old friend who is an Anglican bishop. "I wish we could keep you with us," he wrote, "in the broken 'middle', the place of the cross and the dove." It was not to be. I certainly learned through this terrible time the reality of being broken to the point of despair. I did experience the cross and the dove, without which it would have been impossible to survive. Yet I could no longer find the truth in that Anglican middle ground. Like Newman, when he could no longer sustain his Via Media argument, I had to leave.

In *On Death and Dying* (p. 112) Kübler-Ross quotes from the *Gitanjali.* These are fitting words to describe how we felt as we walked up the aisle at St. George's Cathedral. We were passing out of the experience of denial and isolation, anger, bargaining, and depression into the joy of acceptance. The words have been adapted slightly to fit our situation: "I bow to you all, my Anglican friends, and take my departure. Here I give back the keys of my door, and give up all claims to my house. I only ask for some final kind words from you. We were neighbors for long, but I received more than I could give. Now a new day has dawned and the lamp that lit my dark corner of Anglicanism is extinguished. A summons has come and I am ready for my journey into the heart of Orthodoxy."

6

One Step Enough . . .

I do not ask to see
The distant scene; one step enough for me.
John Henry Newman

I have mentioned that my wife and I were on a visit to India just before we were received into the Orthodox Church. Towards the end of our time there we were in a city called Cannanore on the west coast of South India. It had been a British garrison town in the days of the Raj. Just before I preached on Sunday morning, we sang John Newman's famous hymn, "Lead Kindly Light." It was an unusual choice, but it matched the emotions I was experiencing at the time.

John Henry Newman wrote these words as a poem when he was far from home. Only later did it become a hymn. He composed it on June 16, 1833, on a sailing ship while becalmed in the Mediterranean. He was facing controversy, as we were. He later told people that he wrote the poem because of his concern for the Church of England and its spiritual life. He had been in Rome, and he wrote at the time, "We have a work to do in England." A month after Newman returned to England, John Keble preached in Oxford his famous "Assize" sermon that launched the Oxford Movement. When I sang this hymn in India in 1995, I was very conscious of the fact that there was another work to be done in England. We too would have to go a step at a time.

The Newman poem has a focus on home. Some years after the poem had been published and turned into a hymn, the author spoke movingly of his boyhood home at Grey's Court,

Ham, near Richmond, Surrey. He tells how he looked back on it as a "sort of paradise." Later Newman was to find his home in the Roman Catholic Church.

For us too, "coming home" was a constantly recurring thought as we drew closer and closer to the Orthodox Church. "Home" normally conjures up the happiest of thoughts. I have on my desk a photo I treasure of the home where I grew up, a few miles, as it happens, from Newman's. It still speaks to me of father and mother, of brothers and sisters; it conjures up thoughts of security, joy, happiness, peace, and, above all, family.

Not everyone has the kind of security or family life I was privileged to have, but for most people "home," even if it is only a few corrugated iron sheets in a densely populated shanty town, means something. So "coming home" is a form of imagery that many converts have found helpful over the years.

When the decision was taken to ordain women to the Church of England's priesthood, Dr. George Carey, the Archbishop of Canterbury, urged the so-called "traditionalists" to do nothing quickly but to reflect carefully. This was wise advice. However, from the moment I heard of the decision of the General Synod, I knew I could not stay. The Church of England could no longer be my home. Like others, I had experienced moments like this before, when I had said to myself, "I am leaving." Then I would always change my mind after a good night's sleep. However, this was different. It was an awesome moment when my wife and I, independently of each other, knew the time had come to move.

A week after the General Synod's decision, Bishop Graham Leonard, formerly Bishop of London and now a Roman Catholic priest, wrote an article in *The Times* newspaper (Nov. 20, 1992). In it he said, "A second option is to seek hospitality from the Eastern Orthodox Church. While they are very sympathetic, they are so closely related in this country to the indigenous Churches of which they are part that it is difficult to see this as a realistic possibility."

This article gave me just the nudge I needed to move more definitely in the direction of the Orthodox Church. Dr. Leonard had clearly set his sights on Rome. He called the Orthodox option "unrealistic." If the Orthodox Church is, as it claims to be, the true Church, it must be universal. It must be as appropriate for Britons as for Greeks, for Americans as for Russians. From that moment I was involved in a pilgrimage to see Orthodoxy accepted as an indigenous church in Britain, as it is in many other parts of the world.

In June, 1993, I wrote, at the invitation of the editor of the *Church of England Newspaper,* an article which I called "The Orthodox Option." An important result of this was my introduction to some other Anglican priests who were thinking along the same lines. Some wrote to me; others phoned me. I was drawn, as a consequence, into a small circle of like-minded people. We became known as the "Pilgrimage to Orthodoxy." The days that followed were sometimes painful and stressful, but we found strength and encouragement in one another.

The roots of this fellowship can be traced to the Anglo-Orthodox Society, which for some years had drawn together Anglicans interested in Orthodoxy. One of them, who was to play a crucial role in the Pilgrimage to Orthodoxy, was a priest in Cornwall, Father Charles MacDonnell. He had become increasingly disillusioned with Anglo-Catholicism. In the Easter, 1992, edition of the *Anglo-Orthodox Society* magazine, he wrote a letter asking the question, "What do those leaning towards Orthodoxy do in the event of an agreement to ordain women to the priesthood?"

Another key person had been on the scene for some time already, an American Antiochian Orthodox archpriest, Father Michael Keiser. Father Charles wrote to him in September,

1992, and had a reply a little while later. In January, 1993, Father Michael visited the U.K. and stayed with Father Charles in his vicarage in Hayle, a fishing town in north Cornwall. On Saturday, January 23, he spoke at a meeting in the parish, and he preached the following Sunday.

After the Sunday service they repaired to the Star Inn in Penzance, and over pints of good English ale Father Michael told Father Charles about what was going on in the United States, and that many Episcopalians and others were joining the Orthodox Church. He suggested that the same might happen in Britain, and the Pilgrimage to Orthodoxy was born.

One of the first to be in touch with Father Charles was Father David Sennitt, an Anglican priest in Doncaster, and they both contacted me as a result of my article. The first meeting was organized by an Orthodox layman, Nicholas Chapman, and was held in Moseley, near Birmingham, on June 18. Twenty-two priests attended. I could not be there because of another engagement. The Pilgrimage to Orthodoxy was truly launched.

Father Charles MacDonnell now requested a meeting with two Orthodox bishops, Bishop Kallistos of Diokleia, of the Greek Archdiocese of Thyateira and Great Britain, and Bishop Basil of Sergievo, of the Russian Diocese of Sourozh. A date was fixed, October 28, 1993, and we met in Oxford. Before the meeting the Pilgrimage members had a pub lunch together, the first opportunity I had had to meet them. After lunch we walked to a house just around the corner, and, sitting in a semicircle, we awaited the entry of the bishops.

Father MacDonnell was our spokesman; we were, he said, petitioning to join the Antiochian Orthodox Church and were in touch with the Archdiocese of North America and its Metropolitan, Philip Saliba, in particular. The bishops were clearly uneasy about this proposal. However, we did agree to meet again to give the bishops a chance to share this information with their superiors, His Eminence Archbishop Gregorios, of the Archdiocese of Thyateira and Great Britain, and Metropolitan Anthony, of the Diocese of Sourozh.

Before we met again, a few of us flew to the United States and visited Englewood, New Jersey, to have a full meeting with Metropolitan Philip Saliba. We were warmly welcomed, and Metropolitan Philip made an immediate decision to receive us into the Orthodox Church. Within a few days he appointed Archpriest Michael Keiser to oversee the operation. This filled us with great hope and joy.

Our next meeting with the English bishops was on January 13, 1994. Our plans had raised three major problems for some of the Orthodox in Britain.

The first was the question of which rite to use in the Eucharist. The Antiochian Patriarchate normally serves the St. John Chrysostom Liturgy, called the Eastern Rite. It has also allowed parishes in North America and a few other countries to serve a Western Rite—either the Rite of St. Gregory or the so-called Rite of St. Tikhon. This one is similar to the old *American Prayer Book* service, or the Church of England's 1928 service. Some Orthodox in Britain found these rites difficult to accept.

The second problem was our connection with North America; some Orthodox in Britain regarded this as an intrusion into their own territory. The third problem concerned group receptions. We were petitioning the Orthodox Church not only for our personal reception but also for that of our congregations. This was something new and difficult for the Orthodox in Britain, who up to then had received only individuals.

These problems did not go away immediately, but they have gradually been resolved. First, as it turned out, most of the new Antiochian Orthodox churches in Britain chose the

Eastern rather than the Western Rite. Second, during the summer of 1994 the Patriarch of Antioch himself intervened, and he transferred us to his protection, under the authority of Bishop Gabriel in Paris.

The third problem turned out to be more a practical one than one of principle. The Orthodox Church has received many large groups over the years, the largest being the Russian nation, which converted in 988. Provided each person is properly prepared, there is no reason at all why people should not join in groups of all sizes. If an Anglican parish decided it wanted to become Orthodox, it certainly could, according to Orthodox canon law.

The climax came in September, 1994, when we were invited to go to Paris to meet the Patriarch. We stayed overnight in a hotel at Charles de Gaulle airport. After supper we prayed for our important meeting the next day with His Beatitude. Everything went without a hitch, apart from the fact that two of the men forgot to put their watches ahead one hour for Paris time and nearly missed the bus into central Paris.

The Patriarch expressed himself humbly and simply. He beamed at us and said, "Welcome home." Some of us wept with joy. It had been a difficult time. There had been moments when we wondered if we would ever make it. The barriers had seemed insurmountable. But the arms of the Patriarch were wide open. We were truly on our way home.

Then followed a period of further waiting and frustration, during which we were continually tested by doubts and fears. The Patriarch had said, "Yes." We were welcome. When the father ran to meet the prodigal and threw his arms around his smelly body, the son was not yet home. Welcome, yes, but the last part of the journey was perhaps the hardest of all. The journey of the prodigal from the far country was tough. He had no certainty that his father would receive him. He might have to return to the poverty and deprivations of his adopted home. Yet having been welcomed, the thought of losing this joy was almost too much to bear. So it was for us. The six months between Paris and the first receptions were the hardest. It was too painful to consider that this cup could yet be dashed from our lips at the last minute. However, in the end it all worked out fine.

My wife and I left Bombay, India, on February 13, 1995, and landed at London's Heathrow Airport the following morning. There was still no news. March came, and I was still an Anglican. The first weekend in March, Jeanne and I flew up to Manchester and went on by train to Lancaster. Here we stayed with Father Jonathan Hemmings, now one of our deanery priests, and his family. I spoke to the sixth form of the Lancaster Royal Grammar School, where Father Jonathan teaches. Then we flew to Belfast to meet one of my sisters. From there we went on to Rostrevor. The occasion was the fiftieth birthday party of Gerry Griffin, the wife of a colleague of mine in the Anglican work from which I had just retired. That Sunday, although I did not know it at the time, I preached my final sermon as an Anglican in Kilbroney Parish Church, Rostrevor, founded by the abbess Saint Bronach in the sixth century.

We arrived home from Ulster on March 6, and there was a message to phone Bishop Gabriel in Paris; I was to go over to Paris on Wednesday, March 8, to discuss ordinations. I managed at short notice to get Father Kurt (now Kosmas) Wittwer, one of the men awaiting ordination, to come with me. Then the bombshell hit me. The bishop said, "The ordinations are to start; it is the wish of the Patriarch to set up a British deanery, and you are to be dean. You will also be the first to be ordained." He then went on to tell us that the first ordination was to be in ten days' time.

So here I was, already getting into retirement mode and

having to face a radical change of direction. One of my often-recurring nightmares has been knowing that I am to take an exam next day but having done no work to prepare for it. This was that nightmare come true. The weekend after we got back we went down to St. John of Kronstadt Greek Orthodox Church in Bath, to our spiritual father, Father Yves Dubois, and shouted, "Help!" It is difficult to see how we could have come through the next weeks without the help of him and that community.

Now we had to move fast. I phoned my Anglican bishop, Lindsay Urwin, and made an appointment for that Friday. On that day I handed in my license. It was my official farewell to sixty-four years in the Church of England and thirty-nine as priest. We talked together and then went to his private chapel, where we knelt in prayer. Then the bishop came over and laid his hands on me and gave me his blessing. We embraced. It was a moving moment. I said to him, "Bishop, now I am becoming Orthodox, I realize I will have to get permission to minister in Anglican churches."

"You won't in my part of the diocese," he replied.

As I have said elsewhere, with all its faults, the Church of England must be the hardest church in Christendom to leave.

Things were now moving rapidly. I arranged to go to confession for the first time in my life. I went to Father Gregory of Crawley Down, the superior of an Anglican monastery near us. It seemed appropriate for me to do this. I was going to have to get used to confession in Orthodoxy. However, my Anglican sins needed to be confessed, so I thought, in the presence of an Anglican priest. Finally I went to Father Samir Gholam to make the confession required of everyone before being ordained in the Orthodox Church. My Protestant aversion to confession was being addressed profoundly, to my great benefit.

A date was fixed for our reception and chrismation into the

Orthodox Church. It was to be three days before my ordination in Paris, so I was to be an Orthodox layman for only that time. On March 15, Jeanne and I went up by train to St. George Antiochian Cathedral in London. There, in the presence of a handful of people, we were led by the hand into the cathedral, received, and anointed with oil (chrismated). We had joined the Church that has remained faithful to the apostolic faith for nearly two thousand years. We were now part of the patriarchate that is linked by history with the city of Antioch, where Saint Paul had his base for much of his great missionary work.[1]

So a new mission opened up for us when we least expected it. One thing we have learned from it is that age is no barrier to the will of God. Today it is much more difficult to get a job when you have passed the age of fifty. Yet God does not care how old we are; He always has use for us. As Christians we need to remove the word "retirement" from our vocabulary; it is not in His.

It is not age that matters but vision and dreams. When Joel prophesied the coming of the Holy Spirit, he did not leave old people out. There was provision for them too. "Your old men [and women, of course] will dream dreams" (Joel 2:28). A few weeks before he died, Cardinal Suenens sent me a copy of his last book, called *The Hidden Life* (FIAT publications, 1996). It is about the personal life of King Baudouin of the Belgians. In the front he wrote, "To dear Michael Harper, dreaming dreams together, very cordially."

The cardinal, who moved so many to "dream dreams," is one of the great inspirers of my life. He once invited me over to Malines, when he was Cardinal Archbishop of Malines-Brussels, to spend a day with him. I wrote to him from time to time after he retired in 1979, and he wrote to me also. He was particularly helpful as I went through the difficult time of change that is the subject of this book. He had the gift of drawing people into his dreams, as he did in the last note I had from him before he died.

Yes, my dear Cardinal, we are still dreaming dreams together. You are now in the place where all dreams are also reality. I am in the place where my dreams, of which I have many, have to wait for their fulfillment. So our dreams still bind us together.

1 There may be an ancient link between Britain and Antioch as well. It is interesting to note that St. Eulogius, a priest of Antioch and later Patriarch of Alexandria, in an exchange of letters with Pope Gregory the Great, implies that St. Eulogius himself was instrumental in encouraging the mission of the monk St. Augustine to England.

7

The Witness of Antioch

The Antiochian Church is the cradle of Gentile Christianity, and of Christian missionary enterprise.
International Standard Bible Encyclopedia

When people hear we have become Orthodox, they usually ask us whether we are Greek or Russian. We reply, "Antiochian," and a bemused expression comes over their faces. They have never heard of us before. This is understandable since, so far as I know, we were only the second group of people in Britain ever to become Antiochian Orthodox.[1]

One advantage of the Antiochian Orthodox Church is that we hold the world copyright on the word "Christian." We are told in the Acts of the Apostles that "the disciples were first called Christians in Antioch" (Acts 11:26). The city of Antioch was founded in 301 B.C. by a Syrian leader called Seleucus Nicator and was named after his father, who was called Antiochus. It was one of sixteen cities with that name in the ancient world, all named after the same man. The city enjoyed a perfect situation for trading, just east of the Mediterranean and about 250 miles north of Jerusalem. When it fell into Roman hands in 69 B.C., it became the most important city in the world after Rome and Alexandria. It was called the "Queen of the East"; it was a melting pot and a cultural bridge between the East and the West. It was the first city in the world to have street lights.

Modern Antioch (renamed Antakya) is an obscure town in Turkey, near the border with Syria (it should not be confused with the Antioch in Pisidia—also part of Turkey). A Christian community existed in Antioch from the earliest days of the

Church, though in the fourteenth century the patriarchate left there and moved to Damascus, where it remains to this day. Today our Patriarch, Ignatius IV, is ranked third in the Orthodox world, after the Ecumenical Patriarch (Constantinople), who is "first among equals," and the Patriarch of Alexandria.

Further explanation is needed. After the Council of Chalcedon (in 451) there was a schism in the patriarchate between those who accepted the Council and those who did not. The schism persists, although most misunderstandings have been cleared up and reconciliation and reunion are in sight. To distinguish the two churches, the Chalcedonians or Eastern Orthodox (the one we are members of) often have the word "Greek" in their title. The non-Chalcedonians or Oriental Orthodox usually have the word "Syrian" in theirs. They are often referred to as "Syrian Jacobite."

Although small when compared with the Greek and Russian Orthodox Churches, the Antiochian Orthodox Church has influence and importance that belie its size. Today it is in the forefront of innovative changes in Orthodoxy for which the Orthodox Church is not usually renowned. There is a large church in North America, which has grown considerably in the last two decades; this has been due largely to immigration caused by the twenty-year-long civil war in Lebanon. It is growing also through its absorption of some Protestant churches—Episcopal, Presbyterian, Baptist, Pentecostal, and even one of John Wimber's Vineyard Fellowship churches (more about that later). But our church is also thriving in the Latin American culture, with large churches in Brazil and Argentina, for example. There are Antiochian churches now all over Western Europe, although our strongest concentrations of believers are still in the Middle East, particularly in Lebanon and Syria.

As I now move in Antiochian church circles, I have observed

a truly astonishing fact. The traits so self-evident, according to the records of the New Testament and other early Christian literature, *are still observable in Antiochian Orthodox churches now.* In fact, it is possible to see in Antioch a microcosm of the Orthodox Church in its essence.

Evangelical Theology

The first pillar of evangelicalism is its loyalty to the Scriptures. Antioch, from the very beginning, was a center for that, not least through the preaching and teaching of Saint Paul. The city was also the center of the first major theological controversy, when Jews and Gentiles clashed over a racial question (Acts 11:19ff. and 15:1ff.). The clash was so serious that it had to be referred to the church in Jerusalem, which led to the first Jerusalem Council. When the council was over, its conclusions were sent first to the church in Antioch, where the dispute had arisen.

Antioch continued to be a strong center of biblical teaching, and there developed the so-called "Antiochene theology," which was markedly different from the Alexandrian. Often they complemented each other, but sometimes they clashed. Antiochene theology was historical and exegetical; Alexandrian was mystical and allegorical. The Antiochene tended to expound the Scriptures in their natural and literal meaning; the Alexandrian tended to look for hidden and metaphorical meanings.

The Antiochene school also had a more critical attitude to the Scriptures, regarding some as having more weight than others—an approach that is common among evangelicals in our day. Sometimes there were sharp differences, even accusations of heresy. Yet the Antiochene school never went so far as to be heretical. It produced some great theologians, like Saint John of Damascus and Theodoret of Cyrrhus, and outstanding leaders like Saint Ignatius of Antioch—a key person, as we shall see, whose lifespan overlapped with that of the Apostles. It was, therefore, no accident that when two thousand evangelicals in North America sought to become Orthodox, it was the Antiochian Orthodox Church that received them.

An Evangelistic Church

The second pillar of evangelicalism is its zeal for evangelism. The first church in Antioch certainly had that! The first recorded missionary movement began in this city. In Acts 13:2 we are told that the Holy Spirit said to the church in Antioch, presumably through a word of prophecy, "Now separate to Me Barnabas and Saul for the work to which I have called them." Later they returned (Acts 14:26–28) and reported on their mission to the church at a special meeting. Christian missions began in this city.

The patriarchate of Antioch has always had this strong evangelistic element, which the patriarch welcomed when the North American evangelicals were received. He told them to bring their gifts with them. Also Metropolitan Philip Saliba of North America has always given them his full support. This is especially true of the Department of Missions and Evangelism they have opened to train the Antiochian Orthodox churches in the task of making disciples today.

A Cultural Crossroads

The third great characteristic of the church in Antioch was that it reflected the cultural mixture of that city. As it was an important trading city, businessmen were constantly traveling through it, and people from various places settled there. So in the days of the Apostles there were Jews, Romans, Greeks, and people of other nationalities living and working closely together. There were no ghettos in Antioch; people mixed freely, and the first church there reflected this mixture of cultures.

Although there was much trouble in the other Antioch (in Pisidia; see Acts 13:14), in this Antioch the church always stood firm for racial integration, not least between Jews and Gentiles. This is plain from the account given in Acts 11:19–21. The first preaching of the gospel in Antioch had been exclusively to Jews (see Acts 11:19). But shortly afterwards others came to Antioch who "spoke to the Hellenists [Greeks], preaching the Lord Jesus" (Acts 11:20). From then onwards the church was the means of breaking down barriers and uniting Jews and Greeks and members of other races.

Controversy raged in the Church for some time, and there were attempts even in Antioch (see Acts 15:1) to compel Gentiles to be circumcised. It was because of this that Paul and Barnabas traveled from Antioch to Jerusalem to lay the issue in front of the Apostles in what has been called the Jerusalem Council. The Council decided in favor of the Antiochian view. When the news of the result was made known, we are told that the Antiochians "rejoiced over its encouragement" (Acts 15:31).

In effect, Antioch broke the mold of Jewish intransigence. Because of Antioch, the Christian Church could never be a Jewish sect. It is true that the Apostle Peter saw the initial breakthrough in the house of Cornelius (see Acts 10), but he was later to go back on this. Saint Paul had to oppose Saint Peter to his face, and this was done in Antioch (see Galatians 2:11). It was Saint Paul, not Saint Peter, who pioneered the mission to the non-Jewish world, and his headquarters was Antioch. We have to be fair to Saint Peter: he did redeem himself. It is almost certain that he was the first bishop of Antioch. This would have been unlikely to happen if he had not come round to seeing how essential it was to erect no barriers between Jews and Gentiles.

The Antiochian Orthodox Church of today still has this transcultural flavor, which is special. It seems to be the part of the wider Orthodox Church that adapts most easily to different cultures and transposes itself within those cultures. This is immensely important in the light of the Achilles heel of Orthodoxy—its occasional cultural intransigence, which can encourage petty competition. There is also sometimes a spirit of cultural pride, which could hinder the spread of Holy Orthodoxy in parts of the world where it is at present either unknown or spread thinly on the ground.

Notable Antiochians

We need to mention three well-known Antiochian leaders from the past. One, Saint Ignatius, was the third bishop of Antioch (after Saint Peter and Saint Euodius). The witness of this man played an important part in my becoming Orthodox. I wrote a book some years ago called *Let My People Grow* (Hodder & Stoughton, 1976), which was about Christian ministry. In discussing the subject of the episcopate, I said that the Apostles went into a "smoke-screen, and came out the other side as bishops," and that no one can be sure how the change took place. I had obviously not heard of Saint Ignatius. He became bishop in about A.D. 67, and his life and writings have, more than anything else, convinced me that bishops are not an optional extra but part of the very essence of the Church.

Saint Ignatius was martyred in Rome, possibly in the Colosseum, around A.D. 107. It is important to note that he was born around A.D. 35 and was, therefore, a younger contemporary of the Apostles; the episcopate was clearly regarded as the natural successor to the Apostles. No one ever challenged this position. Saint Ignatius himself was greatly honored, on his way to martyrdom, by Saint Polycarp, who was the Bishop of Smyrna. Polycarp knew the Apostle John and was himself later to be martyred.

Lucky for us, Saint Ignatius had some spare time on his long journey to Rome and wrote a number of letters, seven of which survived him. The Church Fathers often quote them with approval. The authenticity of these letters has been questioned by some Protestant scholars because of the clear indications of episcopacy in them. Professor Lightfoot deals brilliantly with these objections in his book, *The Apostolic Fathers* (MacMillan, 1885). In the second part of Volume I he summarizes his arguments in favor of the view that the letters are authentic. He writes, "No Christian writings of the second century, and very few of antiquity, whether Christian or pagan, are so well authenticated as the Epistles of Ignatius" (pp. 407–9).

The letters of Saint Ignatius are *high church.* They helped me to see that in the apostolic period, episcopacy was well established and intimately linked with the Eucharist. In the Eucharist, according to Saint Ignatius, "the bread is the flesh of Jesus Christ." The bishop is "as the Lord," and without his authority the Eucharist cannot be served. The Church "can do nothing without the bishop." This is the view that still obtains in the Orthodox Church. (Because of the crucial position of the bishop, this point is developed more fully in chapter 13.)

Another Antiochian was Saint Lucian, teacher of the notorious heretic Arius, who caused so much trouble for the Church with his view that Christ was not fully divine. Nestorius, a second troublemaker, also was trained in Antioch. On the other hand, it is interesting to note that the draft of the Nicene Creed was actually compiled in Antioch. It was the Council of Nicaea (and the one that followed in Constantinople) that overthrew the Arian heresy.

The great Church Father Saint John Chrysostom was born in Antioch in 344, shortly after this famous council. He was made a deacon in 381 by Bishop Flavian, and in 386 he was ordained a priest and authorized to preach in the Orthodox cathedral in the city. One of the greatest Christian leaders of all time, he is widely accepted among evangelicals because of his great preaching abilities and his brilliant exposition of the Scriptures in the *Homilies*. In these he used a fresh exegetical style, free from allegorization, which has been a model for evangelicals ever since.

Saint John Chrysostom is best known among the Orthodox for refining the eucharistic rite into the form which bears his name and is used throughout the Orthodox world today. His advice on marriage has seldom been equaled, and he gave a full place to women in the Church, though making it clear that they could not be priests.[2]

Taking Risks

In his autobiography (*Memories and Hopes,* Veritas Books, 1992), the late Cardinal Suenens mentions his encounters with the Orthodox Church. He got on well with Metropolitan Anthony of Sourozh. He writes, "The Orthodox Church needs some daring Davids." I don't know whether the cardinal ever met our Patriarch, Ignatius IV of Antioch, but there is someone prepared to take responsible risks for the sake of the Kingdom of God. He has been at the heart of the spiritual renewal of the patriarchate since he was a young man. This renewal has transformed the Antiochian Orthodox Church since the 1950s. Some of this has involved risk-taking.

Patriarch Ignatius was born in 1921 in the village of Mhardey, near Hama, in Syria. While studying at the St. Sergius Institute in Paris, he was moved by a desire to share the faith. He also wanted to bring Orthodoxy out of its ghetto and to discover living answers to the challenges of modern life. Yet all this had to be consistent with the spirit of Holy Tradition. His thoughts have found expression in his book, *The Resurrection and Modern Man.*[3]

Later he became the founder and first rector of Balamand Seminary, laying a foundation of good leadership through sound spiritual training. Throughout his life he has stressed the need for deep and personal faith. He became a bishop in 1961 and Metropolitan of Lattaquiey in Syria in 1970. He has always been simple, direct, and down to earth. The well-known Orthodox theologian Olivier Clément writes, in his foreword to the Patriarch's book, "His style broke with the former tradition of episcopal grandeur" (p. 15). During the twenty-year civil war in Lebanon, which had such tragic consequences for that country and many of the Antiochian Orthodox believers in it, the Patriarch witnessed to nonviolence and to evangelical love.

He has held the office of co-President of the Middle Eastern Council of Churches, as well as being a member of the Central Committee of the World Council of Churches. As a man of dialogue he has been in the forefront of the discussions with the Oriental Orthodox (non-Chalcedonian) that have made such great strides in recent years. According to Olivier Clément, "This Antioch may well become the laboratory for the reconstitution of original Christian unity" (p. 18).

He was one of the founders, in 1942, of the Movement of Orthodox Youth of the Patriarchate of Antioch. Olivier Clément writes that it was "a prophetic and charismatic movement—from the beginning it worked at the very heart of the Church." According to the thoughts of the Patriarch, change will be possible only by means of a "thoroughgoing renewal of pneumatology and pentecostal dynamism that will conquer the fear and suspicion that the notion 'pentecostal' provokes."

It was Patriarch Ignatius who supported fully the reception of two thousand evangelicals into the Antiochian Orthodox Church in the United States. It is also he who has given his oversight to us and agreed to our reception in this country. Olivier Clément summarizes the Antiochian spirituality of today as having: 1) a great sensitivity to mystery—it is filled with light, a theophany of the Holy Trinity; 2) a great sense of *kenosis* or self-emptying, an act of total love by our Lord felt and expressed by His people; 3) a sensitivity to the mystery of *askesis* (self-sacrifice) and chastity that stands apart from a sensual and corrupt society to embrace values shown in the life of the Virgin Mary and in monasticism; 4) a sensitivity to the appeal of the Old Testament prophets for justice, worked out in the context of the turmoil in the Middle East for so many years.

In the early stages of our journey we were told, "If you decide you want to become Orthodox, you can choose which jurisdiction you wish to be part of." In spite of rumors that we did some "shopping around," our pilgrimage to Orthodoxy from day one was directed towards Antioch. By God's grace and guidance we are pleased to be in that part of the Church that goes back to the Apostles and the disciples who were first called Christians.

1 A man called Arnold Harris Matthew, together with a few of his followers, was received under Patriarch Meletios of Antioch in 1911. He was formerly an Old Catholic bishop, and before that a Roman Catholic priest, having also trained for the Anglican ministry. He drew up a profession of faith and sent it to Antioch.

2 St. John Chrysostom once wrote, "The entire female sex must stand back from so great a task, but also the majority of males" (*De Sacerdotio* 2, 2). See also *Equal and Different* by the author (Hodder & Stoughton, 1994), chapter 11.

3 Published first in French under the title *La Resurrection et l'homme d'aujourd'hui,* Desclée de Brouwer, 1981: in English by St. Vladimir's Seminary Press, 1985.

PART TWO

Being Orthodox

8

The Straight Way

The righteousness of the blameless makes a straight way for them, but the wicked are brought down by their own wickedness. —*Proverbs 11:5, NIV*

"It is gleaming, and leisurely—almost a sauntering pageant . . . priests and deacons, their beards flowing and their long hair uncoiled over coruscating vestments, make processional entrances and exits . . . the old clergy resemble minor prophets." Thus Patrick Leigh Fermor writes about the Orthodox Liturgy he observed in Greece, the country of his adoption. He writes about the heart and glory of Orthodoxy.[1]

This part of the book is about what we are discovering in Orthodoxy, the richness of its teaching and worship. There is a kind of Orthodox "lifestyle" which takes many years to acquire. My words here cannot reflect any of that. All I can do is to share what has struck me most in this period of initiation into the life of a Church which is, in many ways, quite different from the one I have left.

The story and impressions of a convert have interest that those of cradle Orthodox cannot provide. They have never seen Orthodoxy from the outside, nor have they enjoyed the freshness of those first encounters with something that is at once strange and beautiful. New converts know also what they have left behind. They may not yet understand much about what they have joined, but they certainly know a great deal about what lies behind them. This has value as they turn to what seems like a new world. Many cradle Orthodox know about little else than their own particular stream of Orthodoxy.

So in this second part of the book we shall be looking at the Orthodox Church itself—its history, its doctrines, and its life of worship. It is a vast subject, and there are excellent books available which cover the ground more than adequately (see page 200 for some suggestions). Hence this is not to be an academic approach. It is our purpose to share with the reader the things that have drawn us, both on our journey to Orthodoxy and since our arrival in that Church.

The Meaning of Orthodoxy

The Orthodox Church is often referred to as the Eastern Orthodox Church. It is true that the origins of Orthodoxy are to be found in the Middle East, and from there it spread to Eastern Europe. In the Middle East today over ninety percent of all Christians are Orthodox, and in Russia, Bulgaria, Romania, and Greece, for example, the predominant church is Orthodox. The Orthodox Church is the second largest body of Christians in the world. (The claim is sometimes made that the pentecostals hold that position; pentecostals are not one church, however, but thousands of different churches, without a common life or authority.)

However, the word "Eastern" is a misnomer if it is thought to mean that the Orthodox Church is confined to the East. When my wife and I visited Syria in 1995 we met a small group of young Argentineans studying Arabic as part of their preparation for the priesthood. They were members of a thriving Orthodox presence in that country. There are Orthodox churches in China, Japan, Australia, Brazil, and throughout Africa, to name a few. It was largely economic necessity that led Europeans to emigrate to the Americas in the nineteenth and twentieth centuries. However, it was mostly persecution that spread the Eastern Orthodox Church around the world in the same period.

The word "Orthodox" is of much greater significance than the word "Eastern." It sums up well what the heart of the Orthodox Church is and what it has stood for through the centuries. Sometimes when I have told people I am Orthodox, they have looked strangely at me, and said, "You mean Jewish?"[2] Clearly, I am not writing about the general way in which the word is used. I am concerned about the more specific sense as it applies to the Orthodox Church.

In the West the word "orthodoxy" means "correct doctrine." The word "orthodox," according to the *Oxford English Dictionary,* means "holding correct or the currently accepted opinions." The original meaning of the Greek word *doxa* is "opinion." But, as we shall see, it is used in the New Testament very differently—to describe the presence of God.

On the other hand, in the East the word "Orthodoxy" also stands for "correct worship." For the Orthodox, doctrine or teaching and worship are integrally united. In fact, the word "orthodoxy" is translated in all Slavic languages by the word *pravoslavie,* which means "right praise." It is translated similarly in Arabic and other Semitic languages.

The Orthodox Church claims to be the Church that has maintained throughout the centuries, since the coming of Jesus Christ, the true Faith, and has expressed it with true worship. The key Greek word from which the word "orthodox" is derived is *orthos.* It occurs in the New Testament in several important places.

First it describes the healing work of Jesus Christ. For instance, in Mark 7:35 Jesus heals a deaf-and-dumb man who then "spoke *plainly.*" Another interesting example of the healing context is Hebrews 12:13, where the writer says, "And make *straight* paths for your feet, so that what is lame may not be dislocated, but rather be healed." Again, in Acts 14:10, it is used to describe the effect of healing on the crippled man in

Lystra; Saint Paul says, "Stand up *straight* on your feet!"

Then it is used in the context of an argument or discussion, when one arrives at the *right* judgment. "You have *rightly* judged," says Jesus to the Pharisee Simon in Luke 7:43 (see again in 10:28). On another occasion spies from the Jewish leaders flatter Jesus with the words, "Teacher, we know that You say and teach *rightly* . . ." (Luke 20:21).

The word *orthos* is also sometimes joined to another word, as in *orthopodeo* and *orthotomeo.* In Galatians 2:14 Saint Paul writes about the deviations of Saint Peter and others from the truth. He says, "But when I saw that they were not *straightforward* about the truth of the gospel . . ." The notion of "rectitude" is evident even more strikingly in the word *orthotomeo.* In 2 Timothy 2:15 Saint Paul says that Timothy should present himself to God as a workman who "does not need to be ashamed, *rightly* dividing the word of truth." In the Septuagint (the Greek version of the Old Testament) the same word is used in Proverbs 3:6 and 11:5: "In all your ways acknowledge Him, and He will make your paths *straight.*" And again, "The righteousness of the blameless makes a *straight* way for them, but the wicked are brought down by their own wickedness."

We see therefore that the word that forms the first half of "orthodox" is crucial. It speaks of "standing erect," "speaking plainly," "judging correctly," "walking straight," "being on the level," "going in the right direction," and "defining accurately." It is also used in the New Testament to describe the healing power to change what is crooked, devious, and untruthful. The word *orthotomeo* also appears sometimes in an agricultural context. It means to plow furrows in straight lines, from the idea of cutting or carving according to an established rule or norm.

This is what we have found in Orthodoxy. Here is a Church that has not bowed to the gods of fashion, but has walked straight, erect, and on the level. It has spoken plainly and has correctly handled the word of truth. It has gone in the right direction, even when others have elected to go another way. In a word, the Orthodox Church stands for the straight truth and no messing around. In the Divine Liturgy the prayer for the bishops of the Orthodox Church contains the words, "Be mindful, O Lord, of every bishop of the Orthodox *who rightly divides the word of thy truth . . ."*

Right Worship

As we have seen, the word "orthodox" also means "right worship" or "right praise," and the Greek word from which it comes, *doxa,* is one of the richest in the New Testament. Jesus Christ is described in Hebrews 1:3 as the "brightness of [God's] *doxa.*" Jesus speaks of His having brought *doxa* on earth (John 17:4); at the marriage feast at Cana Christ revealed His *doxa* and "His disciples believed in Him" (John 2:11).

Doxa is the New Covenant word for the Shekinah glory. It is a vital word in the Old Testament. There it describes the place where God manifests Himself to His people, as He did, for example, to Moses on Mount Sinai. The Feast of the Transfiguration, when Jesus manifested His glory to His Apostles Peter, James, and John, has held an important place in the Orthodox Church year since the fourth century (in the Western Church it was not celebrated until the ninth century and not widely until the fifteenth century).

It is the glory of Orthodoxy that it has combined the doctrine of the Church with its worship—right belief with right worship. Through many dark days the Faith of the Church has been preserved by the constant and reverent serving of the Divine Liturgy and other acts of worship. The Liturgy has also been a major vehicle of teaching. One can understand, therefore, why the Church is reluctant to change or modernize its liturgies. The Orthodox Church has undoubtedly in modern times, though not always, been weak in the area of evangelism. Its greatest strength has been the richness and variety of its services. Linked to them is the comprehensiveness of the calendar that covers the main doctrines of the Church in depth.

Father Lev Gillet, who died in 1980, wrote many books under the pseudonym, "a monk of the Eastern Church." In one of them he described the Orthodox Church thus:

> Equally far removed both from authoritarianism and individualism, the Orthodox Church is a Church both of tradition and freedom. She is above all a Church of love . . . a strange Church so poor and so weak . . . a Church of contrasts, at the same time so traditional and so free, so archaic and so alive, so ritualistic and so personally mystical, a Church where the pearl of great price is so preciously preserved, sometimes under a layer of dust, a Church which has often been unable to act but which can sing the joy of Easter like no other . . .

Finally, it might have seemed natural to discuss history first; instead I have deliberately placed it after the chapters on the doctrine and worship of the Orthodox Church. The Orthodox Church is certainly "historical." It also worships God who in Christ became man and entered history. Throughout its history, from the Apostles onwards, it has been a Church of right teaching and right doctrine. The Orthodox have been prepared to suffer and die to be faithful to these things. The seamless robe of Christ was not divided by the soldiers, nor has it been possible to divide or separate the doctrine from the worship of the Orthodox Church. That has always been its greatest strength and its most important witness to divided Christendom.

1 *Mani: Travels to the Southern Peloponnese,* Murray, 1958; Penguin ed., 1984.

2 Bishop Kallistos of Diokleia tells a story about a young army recruit in the First World War who joined the Scots Guards. When asked by the sergeant-major what religion he was, he replied, "Greek Orthodox, sir!" He was promptly put on a charge for trying to be funny.

9

Right Belief: A Seamless Robe

We preserve the Doctrine of the Lord uncorrupted, and firmly adhere to the Faith He delivered to us, and keep it free from blemish and diminution, as a Royal Treasure, and a monument of great price, neither adding anything, nor taking anything from it.

The Eastern Patriarchs to the Non-Jurors [1]

In essentials the Orthodox Faith is an unchanging one. Saint John of Damascus once wrote, "We do not change the everlasting boundaries which our Fathers have set, but we keep the Tradition just as we have received it." Right belief is at the heart of Orthodoxy. It is the password to everything.

The Incarnation

It would be a huge task to deal adequately with the whole range of this right belief, even if I had the competence to do it. It has been covered well by Bishop Kallistos Ware in the second half of his book, *The Orthodox Church.* So I am going to concentrate on a single doctrine, the Incarnation of Our Lord Jesus Christ.

There are two reasons for doing this. The first is that it is the doctrine which has most impressed itself upon me since my becoming Orthodox. This doctrine is like a seamless robe, touching the Church's whole life. The second reason is a personal one. When I look back on my life, the Incarnation has not figured strongly in it. Becoming Orthodox is dealing with this deficiency, and as a result I hope I am becoming more balanced and healthy than I was before. Belief in the Incarnation is actualized in the life and worship of Orthodox people, and it touches and explains many aspects of their lives. *Like the seamless robe of Christ, it cannot be separated from any part of the whole; it binds all parts together.*

Now, many Christians believe in the Incarnation, but the belief does not always overflow into their worship, life, and behavior. It is not, in other words, like a seamless robe. A.M. Coniaris writes about this: "If all we Christians do is to look back [to Christ's birth] . . . then our religion is about antique collecting and our Church is in fact a museum. The Incarnation is more than the celebration of an historical event. The same Jesus who came at Bethlehem comes now to anyone who will receive Him in faith, to anyone who accepts Him for what he is, the Son of God and the Savior of the world . . . He comes today, sometimes expectedly, sometimes unexpectedly."[2]

When my wife and I visited the large Umayyad Mosque in Damascus, the Muslim guards were most welcoming when they heard I was an Orthodox priest. This huge edifice was the Cathedral of Saint John from the fourth century; later it was converted into a mosque. All its former ornaments were removed, apart from a shrine where the head of John the Baptist is reputed to be buried and the remains of the baptismal font. The walls are bare.

As I looked around at the magnificent structure, the starkness of it reminded me of some Protestant churches, where there are no icons, crosses, candles, statues, or paintings. Of course, many Protestants believe in the Incarnation, but from the appearance of many of their church buildings one wouldn't think so. (I might add that the interiors of some Anglican churches have more memorials to men and women, many of whom could not be classified as saints, than they have to the honor of God.) The principle of the Incarnation does not permeate the worship of Protestants or dominate their minds. To be fair to them, though, the Incarnation has penetrated other parts of their lives. You will discover this, for example, if you look at the life of William Carey, the great Baptist missionary to India. He had a holistic approach to mission long before it became fashionable in the world of missions. Carey was a man for whom the principle of incarnation was crucial to his understanding of mission, although he was often at loggerheads with his supporters at home over it.

The bareness of the mosque is easily explainable—Muslims do not believe in the Incarnation. They feel bound by the law of the Old Testament that forbids the making of graven images. I must hasten to add that the Orthodox have certainly not canceled the second commandment. Orthodox believe that the coming of Christ in human flesh, although it has not abrogated that law, has changed our approach to it. For God has taken human flesh. We do reject idolatry. For example, icons may not be worshipped. Our veneration of them is addressed *not* to icons themselves, but to the persons represented on them.

Saint Athanasius once wrote, in a letter to Antiochus, "We the faithful do not worship images as gods . . . but our only purpose and desire is to see in the image a reflection of the facial form of the beloved." He goes on to say that if the image on it were removed, we would throw the wood of the icon into the fire as rubbish.

Sir Winston Churchill often used to write to his wife Clemmie from the trenches in the First World War. He would tell her that he took out her photo every night and kissed it before going to sleep. That is what the Orthodox do to their icons.

So we believe that it is not only permissible but God-glorifying to paint icons of the Savior, the Mother of God, and the saints. (You will seldom see any representation of the Father because He has no physical form; He is pure spirit. Here is another important difference between Orthodox iconography and the conventions of Western church art, in which the Father is often depicted as an old man with a long beard.) Orthodox churches are in stark contrast to Protestant churches and mosques—full of icons, color, and the smell of incense. And since God made the senses for man to enjoy, we should use them fully in the worship of our Creator.

Many people would see the Resurrection as the primary focus of the Orthodox. Billy Graham has said that this is the chief influence that the Orthodox Church has had on him; he felt that his emphasis on the Cross needed balancing with emphasis on the Resurrection. My own experience of Orthodoxy is that both the Cross and the Resurrection are stressed and held together in high regard. But alongside these is the Incarnation—the invasion of space and time by the eternal God. God has entered not only our humanity but also the world we live in and the universe of which the world is only one small fraction. The Incarnation is part of God's plan for the salvation of the human race and the whole of creation. It climaxed on the morning of the Resurrection. The plan will be completed at the Second Coming. Then the human race, and the rest of God's creation, will be transformed into the New Heaven and the New Earth.

It is important also to remind ourselves that the Incarnation is one of the major tests of Christian orthodoxy in the New Testament. Saint John writes, "This is how you can recognize the Spirit of God: Every spirit that acknowledges that Jesus Christ has come in the flesh is from God, but every spirit that does not acknowledge Jesus is not from God. This is the spirit of the antichrist" (1 John 4:2, 3). Again he writes, "Many deceivers, who do not acknowledge Jesus Christ as coming in the flesh, have gone out into the world. Any such person is the deceiver and the antichrist" (2 John 7). The Church through the centuries has disciplined those who depart from this truth. Saint John is quite specific: "If anyone comes to you and does not bring this teaching, do not take him into your house or welcome him. Anyone who welcomes him shares in his wicked work" (2 John 10, 11). Doctrinal standards are one thing; the will to enforce them and deal with deviations is another.

Mary in the Orthodox Church

Orthodoxy is very earthy, sometimes too earthy for an Englishman's comfort. It is also full of expressions and experiences of the glory of God. The seamless robe of Orthodoxy holds together this down-to-earth quality with its understanding of "deification." This is the belief that we, sinful and erring people, are called to be *transformed* and made Godlike by the Holy Spirit. So alongside the earthly is the glory of God, and one of the key links is the Orthodox understanding of Mary.

When we touch on Mary, we are coming to the heart of the Incarnation. We are also broaching a cauldron of controversy. For centuries Protestants have been scandalized by the teaching of the Roman Catholic Church on Mary. To some extent their distaste has been justified: there have been those who, in their quest to honor Mary, have given her a position akin to deity. The converse is also true: the failure to honor Mary has impoverished much Protestant theology. Among other results has been the general failure to give proper weight to the Incarnation and a full expression of it in worship and life.

In my search for Orthodoxy I was immediately made aware of the presence of Mary. If you go into any Orthodox church you will always see an icon of the Mother of God on the left-hand side of the royal doors (the doors in the middle of the iconostasis, a screen covered with icons which separates the altar area from the nave). You will see an icon of the Savior to the right. One seldom sees an icon of Mary on her own; she is usually holding her Son, and her right hand is pointing in His direction, as if to say, "Don't worship me, but worship my Son." Mary is always among the worshippers, and her "yes" to God is the prototype of our own response to His call.

In the Western tradition the Mother of God has often been put in a false position. Either we have exalted her beyond measure, almost at times allowing her to displace her Son Jesus Christ, or we have ignored or neglected her, as if Christians had a choice between devotion to Mary and devotion to Jesus Christ. In the Orthodox Tradition we give her a proper place: we neither neglect her nor exalt her inappropriately.

The Western tradition usually calls her "the Virgin" or "the Virgin Mary." She is often represented, either in paintings or statues, on her own. On the other hand, in our Eastern tradition we refer to her mostly as "Mother of God" or *Theotokos* ("God-bearer"). The term "Mother of God" was agreed upon by the undivided Church and recognized at the Council of Ephesus (431). The emphasis is on the word "God," not on "Mother," and the title was used to stress the point that Jesus Christ was fully God, contrary to the views of heretics of that period. These included Arius, who did not accept the full divinity of Christ, and Nestorius, who would not accept the title Theotokos for the Virgin Mary, though the term was never intended as a means of introducing Mary into the divine Trinity.

Here again we see the seamless robe of Orthodoxy. Mary is part of that robe, playing her unique part in the drama of the Incarnation. We see, through the obedience of Mary, our humanity being restored by Christ. As Saint Paul sees Christ as the second Adam, so some of the Church Fathers saw Mary as the second Eve, making good by her obedience the damage done by the disobedience of the first Eve. In the teaching about

Mary in both the Orthodox and Roman Catholic churches, the honor given to the Mother of God is really honor to her Son.

The late Cardinal Suenens had a way of explaining this to Protestants. He told the story of the occasion when he was consecrated bishop. He was touched by the flowers that were sent to his mother. "Do not be afraid of honoring Mary," he used to say. *"Anything you do to honor her will go straight to the heart of her Son."* [3] But we love her as well as her Son. When Jesus said to Saint John at Calvary, "Behold your mother," it was an invitation not only to Saint John, but also to the Church, to receive and honor her. Such honor is given to her not as a deity but as the Mother of God.

Mary and Dogmas

The Orthodox Church does not accept some dogmas concerning Mary that have been introduced by the Roman Catholic Church. We agree with the Roman Catholics that she is "ever-virgin" (more about that later), a title confirmed at the Fifth Ecumenical Council in Constantinople (553), but the Orthodox do not accept the dogma of the Immaculate Conception proclaimed by Pope Pius IX in 1854.

Most Orthodox believe in what the Church calls "the Dormition [falling asleep] of our most Holy Lady, the *Theotokos* and Ever-Virgin Mary." Roman Catholics call it "the Bodily Assumption." The Tradition of the Orthodox Church is that Mary died, as all people do—not voluntarily, as her Son did, but because of her mortality. Like all of us, Mary truly needed to be saved by Christ, but, having died, she was taken up bodily by her Son and already participates in the life of heaven.

The Dormition is not a dogma of the Orthodox Church. It is not mentioned in the Scriptures, which is not surprising, since it took place after most of the books had been written. (It can, however, be said to be scriptural in the sense that something like it happened to others, notably Elijah in the Old Testament.) There are doctrines that belong to the public preaching of the Church, and thus are called dogmas. Examples of these would be the Trinity and the Resurrection. On the other hand, those doctrines relating to the Mother of God belong to the Church's inner Tradition.

Perpetual Virginity?

The perpetual virginity of Mary has for a long time been controversial among evangelicals, though, one must hasten to add, not always and not among all.[4] At the time of the Reformation some Reformers believed in it, and it does not appear to have been controversial. We need to realize that the Reformers were often reacting against the excesses of the Roman Catholic Church at the time, not against the Orthodox Church, with which they had little contact anyway. The teaching in the Orthodox Church on these subjects has been held continuously in the Holy Tradition from early times.

In this connection a frequently quoted text is Matthew 1:25, where the Gospel says of Saint Joseph, "He had no union with her until she gave birth to a son." Some have taught that the word "until" implies that Mary did have union with Saint Joseph after the birth of Christ. That does not necessarily follow. John Calvin points this out in *The Institutes.* He writes, "These words of Scripture do not mean that after his birth they cohabited as man and wife" (vol. 3, p. 71). The Swiss reformer Zwingli says, "She had to be a virgin and perpetually a virgin." And in one of his prayers he refers to Mary as "the pure and ever-virgin Mary."[5]

Others quote the words of Matthew 12:46, which refer to "His mother and brothers" wanting to speak to Christ. However, the Greek word translated here as "brothers" could equally mean "relatives," or it could refer to Joseph's children by a previous marriage, because Joseph was older than Mary according to Tradition. Calvin comments, "In the Hebrew manner relatives of any sort are called 'brethren'. It is, therefore, very ignorant of Helvidius[6] to imagine that Mary had many sons because there are several mentions of Christ's brethren" (*The Institutes,* vol. 2, p. 136).

An American Presbyterian scholar, Dr. Dale Bruner, writes about this: "It is a fact worth mentioning that the major Protestant Church Fathers, from Luther to Wesley, believed in Mary's perpetual virginity. Thus this particular topic does not usually appear on the agenda of Catholic-Protestant talks" (*Commentary on St. Matthew's Gospel,* p. 37). The same scholar, in another book, urges Protestants to give true honor to Mary. "She has the right to bear the names the early church gave her, not for her own sake but for the sake of protecting the full deity of her Son, *Theotokos, Mater Dei* and *Notre Dame.* Mary is the Mother of God into history; this we must boldly confess if we wish to hold to the total deity of Jesus Christ" (*The Christbook,* vol. 1, p. 38).

Where Mary is neglected, as among evangelicals, there will be a diminishing of the understanding and experience of the Incarnation. The overlooking of Mary is also common among trendy Christians. Karl Rahner put it well when he wrote, "For too many people Christianity has become another 'ism', an ideology, an abstraction, and abstractions have no need of mothers." There will also be the rooting of new heresies if Mary is neglected. It is interesting that those churches and people who give Mary her proper place in the Church do not distort the role of women in the Church. Nor do they want to give to them the role of a priest that is symbolic of Christ, who was a Man and not a woman. They reject both sexism, which humiliates women and treats them as humanly inferior, and feminism, which presses for undifferentiated equality for the sexes.[7]

Icons: Honoring Matter

We have noted the central place attributed by the Orthodox Church to the Incarnation. Saint Paul, in his Epistle to the Romans, sees the creation waiting "in eager expectation for the sons of God to be revealed . . . the creation itself will be liberated from its bondage to decay and brought into the glorious freedom of the children of God" (Romans 8:19–21). So the Orthodox Church has always seen the redemption and the care of the creation as linked with that of mankind. Thus church art does justice to the creation, and icons, vital to Orthodoxy, link the two together.

The icon is a "window" to see through. The famous computer software program Windows is user-friendly because of its use of "icons," images that appear on the screen and identify the various computer functions pictorially. Orthodox icons also have a pictorial function, but, unlike the computer program, they are the actual bearers of grace. They are another form of dialogue between heaven and earth, not a monologue or a form of voyeurism.

There were some who wanted to rid the Church of icons, particularly in the seventh and eighth centuries, because they were thought to be a form of idolatry. It was wrong, some said, according to the Ten Commandments, to make any graven image of God. The Orthodox Church holds that the Incarnation has made an important difference. The Word was made flesh. God entered the created world. People were able to see and touch God. So God sanctifies the making of icons to glorify His name.

The great defender of icons, Saint John of Damascus, wrote, "Since God has appeared in the flesh and lived among men, I can represent what is visible in God. I do not worship matter, but I worship the Creator of matter who became matter for my sake . . . and who, through matter, accomplished my salvation. Never will I cease to honor the matter that brought about my salvation!" The Orthodox do not worship icons, nor do they reverence wood and paint. They worship the Christ depicted on icons, and they reverence the Mother of God and other saints portrayed by them.

Idolatry was condemned in the Old Testament. Yet this did not prevent the Israelites, in obedience to God's instructions, from using material objects and images in divine worship. The temple was adorned with likenesses of plants and animals that were not worshipped as idols. As Father Jonathan Hemmings writes, "Absolute worship or adoration *(latreia)* needs to be distinguished from veneration *(proskinesis).*"[8]

Some people puzzle over the look of icons. The faces don't seem alive, as they do in Italian Renaissance art. Instead, they are regarded as being at the intersection of time with eternity; they are dead but immortal. One does need to understand the symbolism of icons to appreciate them fully.

The Orthodox, as we have already noted, are hesitant about representing the Persons of the Godhead who were not incarnated in human flesh. "No one has seen the Father," Jesus said in John 6:46, "except the one who is from God; only He has seen the Father." The world-famous Rublev icon called the "Trinity" depicts the three angels who visited Abraham near the great trees of Mamre (see Genesis 18). Like most icons, it is highly symbolic. Without doubt we were intended to see an allusion to the Blessed Trinity in it. The artist had this in mind, though, strictly speaking, it is not an icon of the Trinity.

My overwhelming first impression of the Orthodox Church has been of a Church supremely concerned to teach and pass on to others "right teaching." Through the centuries it has been worship, particularly in the Liturgy or Eucharist, that has been the chief instrument and expression of that teaching. Let us turn now to that aspect of Orthodoxy.

1 Letter of 1718 in G. Williams, *The Orthodox Church of the East in the 18th Century;* quoted by Bishop Kallistos Ware in *The Orthodox Church,* p. 196.

2 *Creeds for Today,* Light and Life, 1972, pp. 117-18.

3 Quoted in his autobiography, *Memories and Hopes,* Veritas, 1992.

4 In this section I was helped by the paper, "A Journey to Orthodoxy," by Fr. Charles (now Seraphim) Bell, Ph.D.

5 Quoted in *Reformed Dogmatics* by H. Heppe, p. 422.

6 A fourth-century Latin theologian who was attacked by St. Jerome for his denial of the perpetual virginity of the Mother of God. He was seeking to defend marriage against a prevalent overemphasis on virginity. St. Jerome defended the perpetual virginity of Mary in his *De perpetua virginitate B. Mariae adversus Helvidium.*

7 The author has written a book on this subject: *Equal and Different,* Hodder & Stoughton, 1994.

8 In an article, "Images of the Divine," drawn from the book *On the Divine Images,* by St. John of Damascus, St. Vladimir's Seminary Press, 1980.

10

Right Worship: Heaven on Earth

We knew not whether we were in heaven or on earth, for surely there is no such splendor or beauty anywhere on earth. We cannot describe it to you; only this we know, that God dwells there among men, and that their service surpasses the worship of all other places, for we cannot forget that beauty.

Russian Primary Chronicle

The words quoted above come from the report presented to Vladimir, Prince of Kiev, by his emissaries, who had been sent around the world to find the true religion. On the basis of this report, describing their visit to the Church of the Holy Wisdom in Constantinople, he chose Orthodoxy. Very few would dispute that the crowning glory of the Orthodox is their ability, in the words of Bishop Kallistos Ware, "[to perceive] the beauty of the spiritual world, and [express] that celestial beauty in their worship" (*The Orthodox Church,* pp. 264–5).

In the year 612 this great church in Constantinople had 80 priests and 250 deacons. Yet size is not the crucial factor. The same glory and beauty were found in the secret services held in the depth of winter in the Siberian tundra during the communist period. One could give many other examples of this mystery and presence being experienced in small and insignificant buildings all over the world. The competence of the choir helps; the priest's function is important; but when all is said and done it is the Liturgy, inspired by the Holy Spirit, that sparkles with the radiance of heaven.

Orthodox Liturgy

Before we turn to the liturgy, let me explain that in the Orthodox Church the word "liturgy" is used most frequently to describe what other churches normally call the service of the Eucharist or the Holy Communion. Of the many forms of liturgy this, for the Orthodox, is pre-eminent. In this chapter, when I use the word "Liturgy" with a capital "L" I shall be referring to the Eucharist or Holy Communion; when I spell it with a small "l" I shall be using it in the general sense.

In the West we have lived through a period of considerable liturgical change. It has been hailed, both by the Roman Catholic Church and by the Church of England, as a brave new world. Services have been designed to be relevant to modern man. Sometimes scorn has been poured on the old services; some avant-garde clergy and bishops have made fun of them. They have been treated as antediluvian creations, long since past their prime and needing to be consigned to the history books. This is still going on, though now under the banner of political correctness. (Having said this, it should be agreed that the Church of England did need to improve on the truncated 1662 Prayer Book services,[1] and the Roman Catholic Church did require a move towards a less clericalized and a more liturgical Eucharist.)

C.S. Lewis once wrote, "The perfect church service would be one we were almost unaware of; our attention would have been on God" (*Letters to Malcolm,* Bles, 1964, p. 12). In this piece of writing he exposed a superficial approach to liturgy. "There is really some excuse," he wrote, "for the man who said, 'I wish they'd remember that the charge to Peter was "Feed my sheep"; not try experiments on my rats, or even teach my performing dogs new tricks' " (p. 13). His plea, which seems to have fallen on deaf ears, was for "liturgical permanence and uniformity." He called the opposite "the liturgical fidget." There are signs now of a growing awareness that the eviscerated modern liturgies, and the new charismatic services, lack something important—though it is not always clear what that is.

The reform of services has followed the pattern of the reform of doctrine; it has tried to let it all fit neatly with the mind and will of modern man. It has tended to stress the individual rather than the Church, experience rather than faith, modern ways rather than the old paths. As David Mills has put it in the magazine *Sursum Corda,* "There is a sociological explanation why so many clergy like changing liturgies. By constantly revising the liturgy (and inserting his personality) the priest is not only the one who leads the service, but the one who *creates* it. He is no longer just the servant of the Prayer Book, but the master who alone knows the magic words and spells to bring the people to true worship."

One has to say that various objections have been made to Orthodox worship. Some people, for example, complain that it is too "Eastern" in culture and form, and thus inappropriate for Western people like us. I have to confess I failed for many years to take the Orthodox Church seriously. I believed it was meant by God only for people in the Middle East or Eastern Europe. In other words, I thought it was culturally conditioned.

As I moved closer and closer to the Church, I realized what a serious mistake I had made. The Byzantine liturgy is thoroughly Eastern *because it is thoroughly biblical.* We need to be reminded that Christianity, in its origins and essence, is an Eastern religion and the Bible an Eastern book. The foundations of Christian truth stretch back to Old Testament times, and Abraham is our father as well as the father of the Jewish people. Seventy per cent of the Liturgy, for example, is taken straight from the Bible, and other Orthodox services are predominantly composed of biblical texts. I have never yet heard anyone seriously disapprove of the Bible because it is "Eastern" or argue that it is suitable only for Eastern people. Anyone who has a joy and delight in the Bible will relish the Orthodox liturgies.

A second complaint concerns the length of Orthodox services. This can be exaggerated. The Holy Liturgy can be served in about ninety minutes, though it often takes longer, especially at great feasts and at special commemorations. In Russia it can take three hours, but that is exceptional for Orthodoxy. Some years ago a Protestant was remonstrating about the length of the services to an Orthodox priest, who gave a classic reply: "When you are in heaven, what's the hurry?"

What we have often noticed in the Orthodox Church is that little accommodation is made for fashions or human frailties. The Church has not, for example, radically reduced the stringency or length of periods of fasting. Other churches have said, "You can't expect people today to fast like that," and at the Second Vatican Council the Roman Catholic Church reduced the strictness of fasting. The Orthodox Church does not expect ordinary believers to live like monks. It also has a standby provision (called *economia)* which allows for exceptional circumstances. These can be the dietary requirements of diabetics, the needs of pregnant mothers, and the demands of the young, the infirm, and the elderly. Their fasting rules are different from those of others. But the Orthodox Church has maintained a strict pattern of fasting to this day. Whether people observe it or not, most Wednesdays and Fridays of the year are fast days. There are also strict fasting periods not only in Lent, but also in preparation for Christmas, running from mid-November. Then there are periods of up to two weeks at other times in the year.

The overwhelming impression I have of Orthodox liturgy is that it is taken seriously while at the same time it is joyful, with great fluidity of movement. Much Protestant worship lacks action. In Orthodoxy there is none of the light-hearted joking and frivolity so common in modern Protestant and pentecostal services. No attempt is made to make God "popular," to reduce Him to our level and to make Him seem like a "good chap." The Orthodox take everything to do with their Church and faith seriously, and their worship is performed "decently and in order," as Saint Paul put it in 1 Corinthians 14:40. Yet all is done without rigidity or a sanctimonious spirit.

The priest is not seen as "one of us," dressed in a pair of old jeans and a polo-neck sweater. He represents Christ, so he dresses in clothes which make him different from the rest of the congregation. The vestments symbolize the greatness of Christ and His victory over sin and death in the Cross and Resurrection.[2] One day I was talking informally to a congregation after an Orthodox Liturgy, still dressed in my vestments. A wide-eyed young Arab boy came up to me and said, "Father, why do you dress up like Jesus?" That said it all.

Orthodox worship expresses the Christian doctrine on which it is based. An Orthodox service is a kaleidoscope of sights, sounds, and smells, by which we experience the teaching that is the heart of liturgy. It comes to us through our eyes and our noses and our ears.

Orthodox Music

Orthodox music expresses this doctrine in a special way. Normally no musical instruments are used at services. There are no organs in most church buildings. Orthodox people believe that the best way to worship God is through what the Bible calls "our best member," the human voice. It has been said that to sing is to pray twice. In the Psalms the mouth is called man's "glory." So what better way to show forth "right glory" than through that mouth? It also simplifies everything. There are no soloists, because in Orthodoxy there is little room for the exalting of the individual or for performance of anthems or the like.[3] Everything is done with others, as a corporate whole, for the glory of God.

In this section we are able to share only what we have experienced so far in the realm of Orthodox music. This is mainly within the context of the Eastern Rite. First, we have had experience of Russian chanting and then, mostly because of a three-week visit to the Middle East in 1995, of the Byzantine chant. On the whole they do not mix well together, although a few Byzantine numbers have found their way into the Russian music. (The Western Rite music includes Gregorian chanting, plainsong, and the Marbecke setting for the Eucharist, which my wife and I both knew many years ago in Anglican churches. This has more adventurous intervals than the Eastern Rite chant and needs to be learned carefully. There are eight tones in Western Rite music, as in Eastern.)

The Russian chant which we have used has straightforward melodies with simple harmonies (which may or may not be used, according to the availability of singers). The musical scale we are familiar with in the West is used, and intervals between the notes are small. This means that it is extremely easy for all the congregation to follow if they want to. Byzantine chant, on the other hand, is monody (it has one melodic line); it is rich and extremely flexible with quarter tones and often a drone bass. It is very conducive to worship but difficult for a group of people to sing with an adequate ensemble and flow. One must choose one or the other type of chant.

It must be said that both kinds of chant are flexible. If one is uncertain which one of the eight special melodies or "tones" is to be used in the Liturgy, it is always acceptable to intone the words. This is often good to do in any case, because the words always take precedence over the music in Orthodoxy. This is part of the reason why instruments are not used. Nothing should be allowed to intrude upon the freedom to worship through the truths being expressed in the words. In the West we are all very used to being affected by the dynamics, melodies, and harmonies of music. But in Orthodox worship it is paramount that our singing is subservient to the text. This allows the Holy Spirit room to emphasize in people's hearts what *He* wants, which will be different with each individual. "We are very sensitive to the sensual, and watch against its appearance," a bishop said to us recently.

When a BBC Radio 3 interviewer asked a Russian Orthodox priest how he saw Orthodox worship moving in the future, he was speechless at the answer. The priest said, "We want to know more exactly how the first Christians worshipped and more perfectly to worship like them." In other words, the ancient Tradition has stood the test of time, and we cannot improve on that.

A Church for All Seasons

One of the first things that struck me forcefully was the rich variety of the Orthodox Church year. When I was a member of the Church of England I did not take the church year that seriously. Easter, of course. Christmas, naturally. Pentecost, ever since I got involved in the Charismatic Renewal. But very little in between. However, I soon began to realize that the Orthodox take the whole year seriously. For the first time in my life I find that I am entering the key feast days in my diary. I make sure that we observe the seasons of fasting and also the great days of feasting.

To begin with it was not easy to see what it all meant. Yet with the help of books, and having experienced the paramount moments, most things now slot into place. For the Orthodox it is not just the great feasts that matter; everything between is important as well.

C.S. Lewis has a telling section in one of the *Screwtape*

Letters (Bles, 1942, no. 25), an imaginary correspondence between a senior and a junior demon. In this letter the senior demon has to acknowledge how God has skillfully countered the human "horror of the same old thing" with pleasurable changes. He thus balances "the love of change with the love of permanence." So God gives us different seasons, yet the same each year. The demon reports, "He gives them in his Church a spiritual year. They change from a fast to a feast, but it is the same feast as before." This is exactly how we have experienced it—a constant change of tempo and focus, which means there is never a dull moment.

A moving experience for us was to go through Great Lent for the first time. It is called "Great" because of the place it holds in the lives of Orthodox believers. Sadly, in the West, Lent has become progressively trivialized or ignored completely, although it is still taken seriously by Anglo-Catholics in the Anglican Church. When I was a young boy Lent meant giving up sweets. For most people these days it does not even mean that. For many years it had been for me a non-starter. (However, I have to record that I used to give up computer games when I was an Anglican, which was something.)

Some time ago we bought the so-called *Lenten Triodion* (Faber & Faber, 1978), a book of Great Lent services and special devotions. The book extends to about 800 pages, and even then there are omissions, such is the richness of Orthodox life and practice. Orthodox believers take Lent seriously, and our moving through Great Lent, with the Triodion in our hands, has been a voyage of immense joy.

Some complain about the dominant role of the Orthodox priest. It is true that the priest serves the Liturgy (if the bishop is not present). Certain parts of the service are reserved for the priest. He alone is the representative of God and of Christ. But, in fact, most of the services are in the hands or, more accurately, the mouths of the choir and, at least theoretically, the congregation. In some services, like the Divine Liturgy, the people's portion amounts to over seventy percent.

There is a Latin phrase that sums up this vital principle: *lex orandi, lex credendi* (literally, "our faith is expressed in our prayer"). John Meyendorff, in his book, *Byzantine Theology* (Fordham University Press, 1979), writes about this Latin phrase: "The interplay of continuity and change, unity and diversity, faithfulness to a central prototype and local initiative, is unavoidable in the *lex orandi* of the Church. The study of this interplay in Byzantium is a prerequisite for an understanding of its *lex credendi*" (p. 115).

"This inner Tradition," writes Bishop Kallistos Ware, ". . . is preserved above all in the Church's worship" (*The Orthodox Church,* p. 205). The Orthodox take seriously every aspect of worship—its content, its timing throughout the year in the Church calendar, and its shades of emphasis and disciplines, particularly the regular fasting. All combine to encourage us to believe, for worship and believing are closely associated, right worship with right belief.

Worship for the Orthodox is a way of living that has sustained them through centuries of persecution. Let me conclude with the words of the German poet Rainer Maria Rilke:

O tell us, poet, what do you do?
    I praise.

But the dark, the deadly, the desperate
    How do you endure them?
    I praise.

And the nameless?
    I praise.

1 Bishop Michael Ramsey, in the first Constantinople Lecture of Lambeth Palace in 1982, expressed the need for the Liturgical Commission to look at both the *filioque* clause and the Epiclesis.

2 They were probably modeled on the robes worn by the Byzantine emperors when they attended divine worship. Much of the British Coronation service has its roots in the ceremonies of the Byzantine Empire.

3 In small Orthodox churches there may be just the priest and one cantor or reader. But here too the understanding is of a dialogue between heaven and earth.

11

Battered by History

Nothing is sadder than someone who has lost his memory, and the Church which has lost its memory is in the same state of senility.

Professor Henry Chadwick

History is not a fashionable subject; people are becoming less and less interested in it. Gilbert Shaw once wrote, "First men say 'God is dead,' now they say 'The past is dead.' " And, one might add, few are looking for a resurrection. The great motor mogul Henry Ford said, "History is bunk," and many now concur with that succinct analysis. But for serious Christians history is most important. Both the Old and the New Testament are full of history. There are stories of how God has blessed and punished, revealed and hidden Himself, and, finally, how He broke into history in Jesus Christ to change its whole course. *When the Church loses its memory, it is a sign of senility, not of youthful vigor.*

It is important to note that, as I remarked earlier, this chapter on the history of the Orthodox Church has been deliberately placed *after* those on doctrine and liturgy. History has influenced the Orthodox Church, but it hasn't been able to change its essential nature. The Church is like a ship in its relationship to the sea. The ship sails through the sea; that is the purpose of its existence. It is battered by the waves, and may be diverted by storms. But woe betide the ship if it allows the sea to enter its hull. The Church has passed through the seas of history. It has sometimes been buffeted by enormous waves and disappeared from sight, only to emerge a little later, safe and sound. It continues its passage to its ultimate destination in the New Heaven and the New Earth. It is the world that is destined to pass away, not the Church.

The Orthodox Church has sailed through many turbulent waters, yet the "Ark of Salvation" has survived. It is a brilliantly designed ship because its Maker is God. He knew beforehand what it was going to have to suffer. He provided all that was necessary for it to survive and reach its true destination.

As I have said, we live in a world that increasingly despises and ignores history. It is regarded as a boring distraction from the great things of this present life. The history of the Orthodox Church is the history of Christ's continuing presence through the power of the Holy Spirit within His people. God invaded time and history when Christ was born of Mary, and God always works in and through history. The past is not dead, as some believe, because Christ is the same "yesterday, today, and forever" (Hebrews 13:8). He eternally links the past with the present. The present is what it is because it has arisen out of the past. (The Celtic Church too had a truly Eastern and biblical understanding of this. For it there were no clear demarcations between past, present, and future.)

Three Schisms

For the first thousand years of Christianity there was only the One Holy Catholic and Apostolic Church. The Greek-speaking East and the Latin-speaking West had for centuries developed characters of their own, in some ways quite different from each other. In the so-called Great Schism (which was actually a centuries-long process rather than a single event), the Latin church went its own way, pursuing doctrinal innovations that had never been approved by the Church as a whole. From then on the differences increased. The Eastern Church, frequently threatened by Islam, was almost unaffected by the great religious, political, and cultural changes that took place in the West: the Renaissance, the Reformation, and the commencement of the Age of Enlightenment, or Modernity as it is often called these days.

Orthodox Church history has been different from that of both Roman Catholics and Protestants, and the Orthodox Church sees the Roman Catholic-Protestant divide as two sides of the one coin. As Bishop Kallistos Ware has put it, "Protestantism was hatched from the egg which Rome had laid" (*The Orthodox Church,* p. 2). Divisions among Christians have caused enormous harm, and the ecumenical movement of the twentieth century has attempted to address this scandal. These divisions have occurred at roughly five-hundred-year intervals; the first three can be traced to linguistic, cultural, and theological differences.

The first arose after the Council of Chalcedon (451), when the Monophysites separated on the issue concerning the nature of Christ—namely, did He have one nature or two?[1] The Armenian Church, part of this schism, was not represented at all at Chalcedon, as the Armenians were involved in a war at the time. The others became known as the Egyptian Coptic Church, the Ethiopian Coptic Church, and the Syrian Jacobite Church.

The term "Monophysite" was used derogatorily by their opponents, although the churches so designated did seem to believe that Christ only had one nature. These churches did not share in the Greek and Latin culture and language, and it seems that linguistic differences had a stronger influence than theological ones in the controversy that caused the schism. This family of churches is now generally called "Oriental Orthodox" or "non-Chalcedonian."

The second schism had its climax about six hundred years later and split the largely Latin Western churches from the largely Greek Eastern churches. Cultural and linguistic differences also played a crucial role in this, the largest of all schisms, and the most serious and extensive. I will develop this point further in chapter 12.

The third followed about another five hundred years later, but affected only the Western church. The Reformation created the Protestant world, which has, of course, itself split into many different denominations. Finally, some four hundred years later, the pentecostal movement arose and quickly spread around the world, creating its own congregations and ethos.

The good news is that the first great division is being healed. Although the Orthodox Church is not yet in communion with the Oriental Orthodox, rapprochement is close. There is also a new impetus to heal the second major schism. Pope John Paul II has expressed his wish for a major step forward by the start of the third millennium. This is problematic, however, as union with Orthodoxy would require the pope to infallibly declare himself fallible and to give up his claims to universal supremacy, which would undermine his ability to bring his immense flock along with him.

The Early Centuries

There is not space in this book to give a full treatment of the history of Orthodoxy; all that can be done is to point to the main events that have influenced the Church. The Orthodox Church is historic, like Christianity itself; it has lived through the centuries since the coming of Christ to preserve the Faith and to worship the God of that Faith.

The first centuries saw great conflict between the Church and the Roman Empire, leading to immense suffering and bloodshed. All this was suddenly and dramatically changed in A.D. 312. The Emperor Constantine, while traveling through France, is said to have seen the cross in the sky superimposed over the sun, like the Byzantine and Celtic crosses. Under it were the words, *In hoc signe vinces* ("In this sign, conquer"). The following year the Edict of Milan proclaimed the toleration of all Christians. Eleven years later the capital was moved from Rome to the Greek city of Byzantium, which was renamed Constantinople. One of the reasons for the move was that the emperor regarded Rome as too polluted by paganism to be the center of his new Christian empire. In 325 the first Ecumenical Council met in Nicaea. These three events, according to Bishop Kallistos Ware, "mark the Church's coming of age" (*The Orthodox Church,* p. 20).

It is important not to romanticize the Councils, which often met in extremely strained circumstances. It was not unknown for bribery to be employed to encourage support for viewpoints and even for violence to be used. The bishops, some of whom were semi-literate and others old and infirm, found many of the proceedings irksome. Several of them died under the dire physical conditions they sometimes encountered. There were on occasion hidden political and church agendas. But through it all, in an amazing way, the mind of Christ was discovered, and we are today the beneficiaries of those Councils.

Nicaea was followed by six other Ecumenical Councils in the following five hundred years, and these Councils are the bedrock of the faith of the Orthodox Church. We shall see later (in chapter 12) that the Scriptures have always been upheld by the Orthodox Church; that is not in doubt. But the Church has also believed that the interpretation of the Scriptures and the establishing of doctrine are issues for the whole Church to decide. The Ecumenical Councils fulfilled that function. *Only when the whole Church had received what the Councils agreed, and endorsed it, was it deemed that the mind of Christ had been truly discovered. And only then were the Councils called "Ecumenical."*

It has been popular among some Protestants to trace the decline of the Church to the conversion of Constantine, just as they trace its recovery to the Reformation. Such a view is inaccurate and simplistic. It has also justified the almost entire neglect of over a thousand years of Church history, much of which has been formative of history ever since. Some Protestants are also critical of any Church-state relationship. But it has to be said that the relationship between Church and state that followed Constantine's conversion was different from that which developed during the Reformation.

The emperors were never heads of the Church, as Henry VIII and his successors have been of the Church of England. They called the Councils together, and opened and closed them, but had no ultimate control over their proceedings. Some of their appointed laymen did have influence, it has to be said. But when emperors overstepped their authority, there were plenty of Orthodox to defend the Faith. There were occasions when emperors, or senior members of their courts, played a decisive part in the proceedings, but they never drew up or defined dogmas or rejected those that the bishops had agreed. Notable in this respect was the influence of Pulcheria. She was the Emperor Theodosius' elder sister, largely responsible for the calling of the Council of Chalcedon in 451 after her brother, the emperor, had died the year before.

The rise of Islam in the seventh century was to affect greatly the Eastern part of the Orthodox Church, which was to bear the brunt of the conflict and later persecution. Within fifty years of the death of the prophet Mohammed (in 632) his followers had conquered Palestine, Syria, and Egypt, all formerly major centers of Christian life and worship. The rapid spread of Islam continued. Within a hundred years Muslims had reached and nearly captured Constantinople and had converted most of North Africa. They had invaded Spain and had reached into

France until defeated at the Battle of Poitiers. Thus the three patriarchal centers of Alexandria, Antioch, and Jerusalem came under the control of the Muslims, and have remained so to this day. The Byzantine Empire held out for another eight hundred years, but was eventually to fall.

The Struggle for the Icons

One of the distinctive features of Eastern Orthodoxy, as we have seen, is the icon. Icons are usually the first things one notices on entering an Orthodox church building. There is generally a large screen called the *iconostasis,* which separates the altar area from the rest of the church. It represents the line of demarcation between heaven and earth. The royal doors in the center of the iconostasis are decorated with icons of the four Evangelists and the Annunciation, symbolizing the fact that it is the Incarnation and the Gospel which open for us the doors of heaven, through the death and Resurrection of Christ. As we noted earlier, as we face the royal doors, to the right of us is always an icon of the Savior and to our left the icon of the Mother of God, usually holding her Son in her arms.

An important chapter in Orthodox history was the struggle, sometimes at the cost of lives, to keep the icons. I have alluded already to a radical movement that grew up in the eighth century whose followers were called the "Iconoclasts." They demanded the destruction of all icons because of the Second Commandment. They regarded icons as a form of idolatry, as some Protestants do today. The Iconoclasts may have been influenced by both Jewish and Muslim disapproval of representing God (or men and women for that matter) in any visible form, whether by a painting or a statue. The early Puritans were also iconoclasts. As Cromwell's soldiers did in Britain in the seventeenth century, the eighth-century iconoclasts destroyed all depictions of human beings in churches, making the buildings as plain as possible.

The struggle was finally resolved at the seventh and last Ecumenical Council at Nicaea in 787, in favor of the respecters of icons. One more attack followed but was finally defeated in 843; it is commemorated in the Orthodox Church on the "Sunday of Orthodoxy." This is the first Sunday of Great Lent, when the service is normally accompanied by a procession of the holy icons.

Orthodox Christians have a special place for their icons, prostrating themselves in front of them, kissing them, and burning candles or lamps before them. Most Orthodox homes have an icon corner, usually in the living room, which is the focus for family prayer and worship. The icon is not an idol but a symbol, and the veneration is always towards the person depicted, never towards the material icon itself. Only God is worshipped. As one of the great champions of the icons, John of Damascus, wrote, "The icon is a song of triumph, and a revelation, and an enduring monument to the victory of the saints and the disgrace of the demons" (*The Orthodox Church,* p. 34).

The New Jerusalem

There is little doubt that the city of Constantinople, named after the Roman emperor, quickly became a remarkable center of Christian life. The whole city became permeated with the Christian ethos. When the state proclaimed holidays, they were Christian, not pagan. Horse-racing began with community hymn-singing. One is reminded of "Abide with Me," which is sung before the English Cup Final at Wembley, or of the Welsh singing of "Cwm Rhondda" at Cardiff Arms Park before a rugby match.

Even in the business world contracts were signed with the

cross, and theology was a major source of conversation. It became almost too much for Saint Gregory of Nyssa, who once complained, "If you ask 'Is my bath ready?' the attendant answers that the Son was made out of nothing." The Church in this city, and in the rest of the Byzantine Empire, earned a good reputation for caring for the poor and needy; many bishops gave their entire financial resources to this end, and the teaching and example of men like Saint John Chrysostom are well documented.

Monasticism also thrived in this period, when the whole of social and political life was flavored with the Christian gospel. As we have mentioned, Christianity began to spread after the conversion of Constantine. As Christians acquired greater economic freedom, and some became prosperous, the witness of the monasteries became increasingly important. As Bishop Kallistos Ware points out, the society of that day "ran the risk of identifying the kingdom of God with an earthly kingdom. The monks by their withdrawal from society . . . fulfilled a prophetic and eschatological ministry in the life of the Church. They reminded Christians that the kingdom of God is not of this world" (*The Orthodox Church,* p. 37).

The Byzantine period saw a sensitive, but often misunderstood, relationship between Church and state (if I may say so, a much better one than the models developed later by Protestants in the aftermath of the Reformation). The emperor had his sphere, in which he had absolute power, and the Church, under the bishops, had hers. Yet the life of the Empire formed a unified whole, and the line between Church and state, though fixed, was never rigidly enforced. They were not identical, nor was one considered superior to the other. As Bishop Kallistos Ware writes, "The two were seen as parts of a single organism" (*The Orthodox Church,* pp. 40–41). With a few exceptions this harmonious partnership, based as it was on mutual respect, remained intact until the end of the Byzantine Empire with the conquest of Constantinople by the Turks in 1453. But this partnership was to be shattered by the tragedies of schism, war, and persecution.

1 I have explained the term "Monophysite," and the misunderstandings concerning it, earlier in the book; see chapter 3, note 7, p. 54.

12

Schism, Evangelism, and Martyrdom

The polluted altars, the sacred vessels stained with blood, the ravaged religious houses too eloquently declared the end of Christian unity.
Nicholas Zernov on the sack of Constantinople by the Crusaders, 1204[1]

The preachers of materialism and atheism, who proclaim man's self-sufficiency, are preparing indescribable darkness and horror for mankind under the guise of renovation and resurrection.
Fyodor Dostoevsky [2]

One of the greatest tragedies of history was the split between the Western Church under Rome and the Eastern under Constantinople. In the summer of 1054, a trio of men filed into the great Church of the Holy Wisdom in Constantinople and placed a Bull of Excommunication on the altar. One of them, Cardinal Humbert, shook the dust from his feet as he left and said to the astonished congregation, *"Videat Deus et judicat"* ("Let God look and judge"). True words: He has looked and He has judged.

Exactly how it happened is still one of the unsolved mysteries of Church history, a whodunit on a vast and deeply tragic scale. The seeds had been sown at least five centuries earlier. There was no clean break in 1054; this is a common mistake. In fact, there never was an exact moment of fracture. The Eastern and Western churches drifted apart for the next four centuries; the so-called "Great Schism" took nearly four hundred years to be completed.

The details we have about the events of 1054 may help us to understand why no one at the time took them seriously. For one thing, Pope Leo IX died in May of that year while imprisoned by the Normans, so it is difficult to see by what authority Cardinal Humbert issued his excommunications. The Patriarch (Michael Cerularius) refused to accept the credentials of the papal legates once he heard that the Pope had died.

It seems clear also that there was a massive clash of personalities between the Patriarch, who was narrow-minded and hot-tempered, and the Cardinal, who was hard-headed and aggressive. In the words of Nicholas Zernov, the accusations were "misinformed, trivial or baseless." (One, for example, was the unwillingness of the Patriarch to baptize women in labor.)

The *filioque* clause was a point of contention. Rome accused the Eastern Church of the willful corruption of the Nicene Creed by the deletion of the word *filioque.* Apparently the Cardinal was so ill-informed, he did not even know that the original creed did not include the *filioque* clause. The word *filioque* is connected with important principles that are as relevant today as they were in the century when the Great Schism took place. The controversy has two major aspects. One is doctrinal; the other concerns the way the Church arrives at doctrinal definitions.

Filioque in Latin means "and the Son." The word was added to the Nicene Creed where the Holy Spirit is described as "proceeding from the Father." This addition first occurred in Spain in the sixth century. Though initially condemned by the pope of Rome, it gradually took hold throughout the Latin churches. It was to take another five hundred years before the issue split the Orthodox and Roman Catholic churches, although there were a number of temporary breaks in communion. The most notable of these centered on Photius, who was Patriarch of Constantinople from 858 to 869 and 877 to 886.

The doctrinal question involves our understanding of the "procession of the Spirit." The issue concerns the nature of the Holy Spirit, not His activity. The key Scriptures, which the Church Fathers followed, are John 14:26, "But the Helper, the Holy Spirit, *whom the Father will send in My name,* He will teach you all things. . ." and John 15:26, "But when the Helper comes, *whom I shall send to you from the Father, the Spirit of truth who proceeds from the Father,* He will testify of Me."

The Nicene Fathers used the verb translated "proceed" to describe the relationship between the Father and the Spirit in the same way as they used the verb translated "beget" to describe that between the Father and the Son. They needed to protect the fact that the Persons of the Trinity are "co-equal" and "co-eternal." The Council of Nicaea saw the Father as the "head" of the Trinity, and the Son and the Spirit were begotten and proceeded in their Persons eternally from the Father. The addition of the phrase "and the Son" threw the whole relationship out of balance and produced grave repercussions later.

But there was another aspect to this controversy that raises a matter of principle. The Orthodox Church quite rightly said something like this: "Wait a moment. Did not the Nicene Fathers of both the East and the West define this doctrine and agree on it together? How is it that one section of the Church decided to change it without the agreement of the whole?" I think this is a vital question which will not just go away. It is one of the reasons why some Orthodox describe the Roman Catholic Church as the "first Protestant Church." At the Third Council of Toledo in 589 one small part of the Church decided unilaterally to change the Nicene Creed. A thousand or so years later, at the Reformation, another group of Christians decided to declare their independence. The Protestant denominations were born, and were soon to split into hundreds of other denominations, because they decided to interpret truth in their own way without reference to the ecumenical Tradition of the Church.

The Orthodox Church rightly maintains that any doctrine as important as the nature of the blessed Trinity has to be agreed upon by the whole Church. This was done at the first seven Ecumenical Councils of the undivided Church. To add to or subtract from this doctrine is to be party to heresy and to risk schism in the Church. To go wrong here will lead quickly and inevitably to other errors.

Since 1054, the churches of the East and West have drifted further and further apart. The Orthodox Church maintains clearly that Christ is the Head of the Church. Bishops are "first among equals," as the Father in heaven is in His relationship with the Son and the Spirit. Orthodox historically accepted the See of Rome and the pope as first among equals, but cannot accept the pope's infallibility or his absolute rule over the Church.[3]

Much progress has been made in this century towards reconciliation between Orthodoxy and Catholicism. The anathemas they directed at each other in the eleventh century have been withdrawn. There is growing agreement in many areas, and a great deal of overlap in doctrine and practice. Yet centuries ago, with the division of the two empires under separate emperors and the break-up of the unity of the Roman Empire compounded by the invasion by the barbarians from the north of Europe, unity became strained, and it was more difficult to resolve the theological issues that were surfacing. The rise of Islam was a challenge to the whole Church, but it was the Eastern Church that had to bear the brunt of it. Several attempts were made to restore communion, but the activities of the Crusaders made this a great deal more difficult, as we shall see.

The Crusades

The schism that had taken place over theological issues, and had been restricted largely to the higher levels of the Church, became deeply emotional and reached a popular level through the Crusades, a form of Western imperialism that was directed mainly against the Jews and the Muslims. It was an early form of ethnic cleansing, which caused resentment that remains to this day in the Middle East. Yet many people are unaware of the fact that the same imperialism was directed by the Western Church against the Eastern Church.

As the Crusader armies poured across the Middle East, they began to interfere with the life of the Church in an early type of proselytism. They removed Greek bishops from office and appointed their own Latin ones. Worse was to follow. In 1204 the Fourth Crusade turned aside to attack Constantinople. There followed three days of murder, vandalism, and rape. Nothing was spared; churches, monasteries, libraries, and private homes were sacrificed. This outrage deepened schism to an unbridgeable abyss. National hatred now replaced theological argument. Sir Stephen Runciman has written, "The Crusaders brought not peace but a sword; and the sword was to sever Christendom" (quoted in *The Orthodox Church,* p. 60). The myth of Crusader piety in the West needs to be exploded. They did immense damage throughout Eastern Europe and the Middle East. It should be added, however, that there has always been fault on both sides, and God has given us, through repentance and forgiveness, a divine route to reunion.

A Golden Age of Missions

Some of what has gone before, in this brief survey of

Orthodox history, may have left a bad taste in the mouth. However, we can now move to something better. It is one of the greatest and most significant moments in Church history and concerns the work of two of the world's most renowned missionaries, Saint Cyril and Saint Methodius. (Pope John Paul II honored them as co-patrons of Europe with Saint Benedict from the Western Church.) The visionary for their historic evangelism was a Patriarch of Constantinople called Photius; Cyril and Methodius were appointed by him to the task of bringing the gospel to the Slavs in Moravia, Bulgaria, Serbia, and Russia. Cyril had the great advantage of being a brilliant linguist and fluent in the Slavonic dialect of the Macedonian Slavs, which was understandable to the other Slavic tribes.

Cyril and Methodius began their work in Moravia (modern Czechoslovakia) by inventing an alphabet for Slavonic (called the Cyrillic alphabet) and translating the Scriptures and services into this tongue, in which many Slavs worship to this day. Thus Eastern Europeans were able to worship in a language they understood, something that was denied to most Christians in Western Europe. This is another example of the Eastern Church adopting a principle that was to be taken up much later by the Protestant reformers in the sixteenth century. Pope John Paul II acknowledged the importance of the work of Cyril and Methodius in his encyclical on unity, *Ut Unum Sint.* "They put into practice," the Pope writes, "that perfect communion in love which preserves the Church from all forms of particularism, ethnic exclusivism or racial prejudice, and from any nationalistic arrogance."[4]

Cyril died in 869 and Methodius in 885. They passed away before the fruitfulness of their mission became apparent. The Western Church eventually eradicated all traces of what they had done in Moravia—some of their followers were expelled from the country and others were sold into slavery—but within a hundred years, encouraged by the labors of these two men, the foundations were to be laid for successful Slavic missions in Bulgaria, Serbia, and Russia itself. Eventually Orthodoxy also spread into Romania, which was primarily Latin rather than Greek or Slavic in language and culture. Truly, the work of Cyril and Methodius has borne great and good fruit in Eastern Europe.

Radiance in Conflict

The Orthodox Church has had a divine call to suffer, beyond anything experienced by Christians in the West. Since the seventh century, at any given time large parts of the Orthodox world have been under persecution from either Islam or communism; no Orthodox country has completely escaped from both. The Church has been, in a literal sense, a church of martyrs. It has had, over the centuries, millions of martyrs who have died rather than renounce their faith—more in this century than in all the first four centuries put together. Recent years have been a particularly dangerous time for Christians to live in, especially in Eastern Europe and the Middle East.

In the early centuries martyrdom was common, and many Christians knew from their baptism that their lives could be very short. Emperor Constantine's conversion and the cessation of persecution in the Roman Empire gave a great impetus to monasticism. The calling to be a monk or a nun was regarded as a new form of martyrdom. It replaced the physical and violent forms that had so often marked the early centuries. In this too the Eastern Orthodox Church led the way. The practice of monasticism began in the East, led by the Desert Fathers, of whom Saint Anthony was probably the first (251?–356). It has continued ever since. Mount Athos, the holy mountain overlooking the Aegean still occupied by over a thousand monks, is the symbol of that strong tradition. Eastern monasticism differs from Western in that it has no religious orders, such as Benedictines, Franciscans, etc.

It seems that history has come full circle. In the early centuries the Church was a small, persecuted minority, living often in a hostile environment, having to conduct its life under perpetual harassment and threat. In our day the Orthodox Church has had to live through a similar experience in Eastern Europe and the Middle East. In both the Roman Empire under some emperors, particularly Diocletian, and in the evil empire of communism, particularly in the Soviet Union, Christianity has been oppressed and Christians treated as criminals. Yet the Church has not only survived; it has triumphed and grown in the process.

The suffering of Orthodox believers in the twentieth century exceeds anything before in Church history. Many of their stories are known only to God; some may emerge in the future as more is known about the terrors of communism. From October 1917 until the end of the 1980s, the most vicious and scientifically controlled persecution the Church has ever faced was the experience of all Christians in Russia, particularly the largest and most influential group, the Orthodox. After the Second World War this persecution was to be experienced in countries like Bulgaria, Romania, Yugoslavia, and Albania as well.

The unambiguous purpose of the atheistic Communist State was to wipe out the Church altogether by whatever means necessary, however gruesome and vile. A few clips of film show this, and one is firmly fixed in my mind. There are some Orthodox believers who are carrying icons out of a church building, which is presumably due to be demolished or converted into a tractor garage. They are being mocked and spat on, their bodies manhandled, the icons struck and vilified. Yet they carry on without striking back: one event in thousands caught on camera, a window on a period of unprecedented human suffering.

The persecution of bishops, priests, monks, and nuns was intense. No one knows the full account, but figures would suggest the number of bishops murdered exceeded 200 and that of priests over 40,000. The laity died by the millions, and the Russian Orthodox Church was to go through a crucible that was to purify the Church in a remarkable way. With a rare combination of bravery and humility, they survived and were victorious over the worst the communists could throw at them. The joyful cry reverberated throughout this dark period, "Christ is Risen! He is risen indeed!" The paschal hope sustained the Orthodox people through their crucifixion.

An interesting example of what happened during the Soviet period is recounted in the book by Dimitry Pospielovsky, *The Russian Church under the Soviet Regime 1917-1982.*[5] The city of Odessa, with a population of half a million, had only one church open. Even this was a concession. Stalin's eye specialist was the famous Filatov, a practicing Orthodox believer, who asked, in return for his treatment of Stalin's eyes, for this church to remain open. Stalin agreed. But there was no resident priest. Once a year (at Easter) a priest who had been in hiding would show up from the crowd. After the service he would be arrested and never seen again. This went on until all the priests who dared martyrdom had disappeared. So the deacons took over, although unable to serve the Liturgy itself, until they too disappeared. They were replaced by readers, until these were liquidated. "In the last few months before the German attack there remained only laymen, who prayed the best they could in the church."

The theologian Vladimir Lossky, in his book *The Mystical Tradition of the Eastern Church* (London, 1957, p. 149), documents remarkable happenings, including the renewal of icons.

Often in Russia during this period old icons were miraculously made new and fresh. "In every place," Lossky writes, "where the faith has been put to the test, there have been abundant outpourings of grace, and the most astonishing miracles." He goes on to describe the scene: "All this was scarcely noticed. The glorious aspect of what had taken place in Russia remained almost without interest. . . . The crucified and buried Christ will always be judged thus by those who are blind to the light of his Resurrection."

The annals of the Orthodox Church, so cruelly battered by its history, abound in the feats of self-sacrifice and heroism of her saints. I want to focus on one in particular, the New Martyr Elizabeth.

The Example of a Saint

Until recently not much has been known about the Grand Duchess Elizabeth. She was vilified, first by some who resented her marrying into the Russian royal family, and then by the communists, who tried to expunge all records of her life after they murdered her in 1918. So, until comparatively recently, we have known little about the life and work of this remarkable woman. Just as this book was being finished new material became available through the publication of the book, *A Lifelong Passion: Nicholas and Alexandra—Their Own Story.*[6] This book contains unpublished material from the former Soviet archives in Moscow about the Romanov family. Although principally about Tsar Nicholas II and his wife Alexandra, it includes new material about the Grand Duchess Elizabeth as well. Other books and material are available.[7]

The Grand Duchess Elizabeth was a favorite granddaughter of Queen Victoria. She carried on a lively correspondence with the Queen, which can be found in the Royal Archives at Windsor. The Grand Duchess Elizabeth was born the second child of the Grand Duke Louis IV of Hesse-Darmstadt and Princess Alice, the daughter of Queen Victoria. Her elder sister Victoria married Prince Louis of Battenberg. (Their son was the late Lord Louis Mountbatten, the last Viceroy of India, a Second World War hero and a close friend of the British royal family.) Her younger sister Alix married Tsar Nicholas II of Russia and was murdered at Ekaterinburg by the communists in 1918, with the tsar and their five children.

Elizabeth grew up a strikingly beautiful woman and was courted by the German Kaiser Wilhelm. She turned him down. In 1884 Queen Victoria gave her assent to Elizabeth's engagement to Grand Duke Serge Alexandrovich, the brother of Tsar Alexander III of Russia. Elizabeth was nineteen years old and deeply in love. They were married in the chapel of the Winter Palace in Saint Petersburg.

The Grand Duchess Elizabeth was baptized a Lutheran, as were all the members of the German Royal Houses. The man she married, the Grand Duke, was a devout member of the Russian Orthodox Church. No pressure was brought on her to convert, either by the Grand Duke or by any other members of the royal family. She was given complete freedom to worship as a Lutheran.

It was on a visit to Jerusalem (where she was later to be buried) in October, 1888, that she decided to become Orthodox. This was a move which was strongly objected to by her father in Germany (her mother had died some years earlier). She made it plain that she wanted to do this out of personal conviction, not simply to please her husband and his family.

In 1891 her husband, Grand Duke Serge, was appointed Governor-General of Moscow, where there was considerable political unrest and bloodshed. On February 17, 1905, the Grand Duchess became a widow. Her husband was instantly killed by a terrorist bomb which exploded on his chest. His assassin, Ivan Kalyaev, an anarchist, was arrested by the police, shouting as he was dragged away, "Down with the Tsar! Long live the Revolution!"

Three days later Elizabeth went to the Taganka prison and told the governor that she wanted to see Kalyaev. She asked that this be kept secret and divulged to no one; her wish was not honored, and many false rumors spread around Moscow as a result. The Grand Duchess was deeply distressed that the visit became known to the public. She felt no hatred for the man who had murdered her husband, but she wanted him to repent of his crime and ask for God's forgiveness. She stayed only a very short time in his cell and there was no political discussion.

When she entered the cell, the man asked who she was, and she replied, "I am the wife of the man you have killed. Why did you do it?" Kalyaev was moved by her visit but maintained he did it because of his principles. She left a small icon in the cell and asked a warder to let her know whether Kalyaev kept the icon or destroyed it. Kalyaev was defiant to the end and was hanged in May of that year. Later at the site of the crime Elizabeth had a cross erected with the words, "Forgive them, Father, for they know not what they do." Lenin was later to destroy this monument.

About a year after she became a widow, Elizabeth gathered her considerable collection of expensive jewelry, including her wedding ring. She gave some to the State, some to her family, but most of it went to the founding of the convent of Saints Martha and Mary. One of the criticisms of the Moscow Synod, before the new community was recognized, was the fact that Martha came before Mary in the names she chose for it. This was not a mistake but deliberate. "Martha," the Grand Duchess explained, "had not been treated fairly in church tradition. Christ did not condemn her. He knew that her solicitude was an expression of her love for him. He merely warned her not to be carried away by domesticities" (*An Unbroken Unity*, p. 63).

It took a long time to get her community recognized. In the end it needed the intervention of the tsar himself and an imperial decree to get the community established. In April, 1910, Archbishop Triphonius gave the veil to Elizabeth. Then the first twenty young women, from the richest to the poorest families in Russia, became the founding sisters of the new community. Their whole work was to care for the poor and needy in Moscow, of which there was no scarcity.

In 1917 the Russian Revolution broke out, and the following year the Grand Duchess Elizabeth was arrested along with the rest of the Russian royal family. The tsar and his family were taken to Ekaterinburg, where they were later all murdered and their bodies thrown down a mine shaft. Elizabeth, however, was taken to Alapaevsk. There she and others in her party, including the faithful Sister Barbara, also to be canonized, were murdered on the night of July 18, 1918.

According to the communist archives recently published, they were taken at night outside the building where they were staying on the pretext of an armed attack. No one was to see them. Outside the house their hands were tied behind their backs and they were blindfolded. Their assassin's name was Ryabov. The tsar's family at Ekaterinburg had all been quickly shot or bayoneted to death on July 16. However, a worse fate awaited the Duchess Elizabeth and some of her companions—they were thrown alive down an abandoned mine shaft.

Some died almost immediately. Others, including the Grand Duchess, had to endure a slow and lingering death in horrifying circumstances. After they were thrown down the mine shaft, hand grenades were hurled at them by the guards. Some died, but others, including the Grand Duchess Elizabeth, lived for a time and died eventually from their injuries and exposure. Eyewitnesses said they heard the Cherubic Hymn sung from the bottom of the shaft, the singing led by Elizabeth herself.[8]

Shortly after these events, the White Army, which was fighting the communist Red Army, recaptured Alapaevsk, and the bodies were recovered. The Whites found two unexploded grenades beside the body of the Duchess Elizabeth, which was unharmed by the explosions.

There was another remarkable chapter to this story. In Moscow some Russian businessmen had supported the work of Elizabeth. One of them had a son who was a priest, and he happened to be in the area when the bodies were recovered. Father Seraphim made a vow that he would arrange for the bodies of Elizabeth and her companion Barbara to be transported to Jerusalem for burial. He had little understanding of geography, but he knew he could not go west because Russia was firmly in the grip of the communists. So he decided to smuggle the two coffins eastwards to Peking in China, where there was an Orthodox mission.

The journey took two years and was an adventure in itself. In Peking the coffins had to be changed, and the body of Elizabeth was found to be uncorrupted. According to eyewitness accounts, "She looked asleep" (*An Unbroken Unity,* p. 130). The three fingers of her right hand were folded as if she had been trying to cross herself. From China the coffins were taken to Jerusalem to be buried finally in the Church of Mary Magdalene on the Mount of Olives in 1921. When Saint Elizabeth's coffin was opened in 1982, eyewitnesses told how the room filled with the fragrance of "something like honey and jasmine." Her body was mostly incorrupt.[9]

This is the story of a famous person who became a saint. Her biographer writes, "Her breath was stilled at the bottom of a disused mine shaft in Siberia. But a life like hers gains eternity, even when considered through the lens of time" (*An Unbroken Unity,* p. 137). How many millions of others died unnoticed and uncared for in those awful days of communist rule? As Tertullian once said, "The blood of the martyrs is the seed of the Church."

1 *Eastern Christendom,* Weidenfeld & Nicolson, 1963, p. 107.
2 *A Writer's Diary,* 1873.
3 Olivier Clément writes, "It was [the Church in] Antioch which from the beginning knew how to properly define the role of Rome." In his foreword to *The Resurrection and Modern Man* by His Beatitude Patriarch Ignatius IV of Antioch and all the East, p. 17.
4 p. 25. He quotes from the encyclical *Slavorum Apostoli.*
5 St. Vladimir's Seminary Press, 1984, p. 175. The story was told to the author by a Russian Orthodox priest who lived in the area during that period.
6 Weidenfeld & Nicolson, 1996. The records have been put together by Andrei Maylunas and Sergei Mironenko, who is director of the State Archives of the Russian Federation.
7 Books which refer to her life and work include *An Ambassador's Memoirs,* by Maurice Paléologue (Hutchinson, 1923-5, 3 vols.; one-volume edition, 1973); he was the last foreign ambassador at the court of the tsars of Russia, and his account of the last years of the Romanovs is regarded as being accurate. *An Unbroken Unity,* E. M. Almedingen, Bodley Head, 1964. A more recent biography is *Grand Duchess Elizabeth of Russia* by Lubov Millar (translated from the Russian), Nikodemos Orthodox Publications Society, 1991.
8 The communist report clearly states this. It recalls, "Then from beneath the ground we heard singing! I was seized with horror. They were singing the prayer, 'Lord save your people.' "
9 On September 14, 1996, while on a visit to our Orthodox Church of the Holy Cross in Lancaster, I met a Russian Orthodox man called Mr. Spyridon Stewart who happened to have been one of these witnesses. He told us that he saw the Grand Duchess's body in a glass coffin in a church on the Mount of Olives near Jerusalem. He confirmed to us the body was largely incorrupt.

13

Can I Be Orthodox and Evangelical?

Whatever would possess two thousand Bible-believing, blood-bought, Gospel-preaching, Christ-centered, lifelong evangelical Protestants to come to embrace this Orthodox faith so enthusiastically?

Father Peter Gillquist [1]

We had heard vague rumors about the conversion of many evangelicals in the United States to Orthodoxy. At first it was hard to believe, particularly since they came from the far right of the evangelical spectrum. When the rumors were confirmed we took heart. Up to then I had not met a single evangelical who had become Orthodox, and perhaps even thought the two were incompatible.

When the Grand Duchess Elizabeth, whose story we have just recounted, looked at Orthodoxy for the first time through her Lutheran eyes, it was said that "all of it together at once repelled and compelled her." Many evangelicals have reacted in the same way. There are many outward features of the Orthodox Church that put evangelicals off. There are the vestments, for example, that priests wear. When I was ordained a deacon in Southwark Cathedral on Trinity Sunday, 1955, I refused to wear a stole. I remember Archdeacon Leslie Brown (later to become the bishop of Birmingham) standing at the entrance to the cathedral with stoles over his arms. He was vainly hoping to persuade us, even at the last minute, to wear one. I resisted temptation.

Then there are the various rituals associated with the services: crossing oneself (which the Orthodox do frequently), reverencing icons, kissing the hand of the bishop, and burning incense. Evangelicals span a whole range from the simplicity of Baptists to the modest rituals of Anglicans. But Orthodox ritual takes things a stage further than any evangelical I know is willing to go.

But when one looks deeper, one sees that the core of the Orthodox witness is remarkably evangelical in its essence. Once one has come to terms with the central features of the Orthodox Church, the rest follows quite easily and naturally.

In my earliest recollections of having a serious faith I was clear, and often dogmatic, about the essentials of the faith and what one looked for in the Church. The first essential, the impact of which I am still aware of, was the Bible. I was for a time a *sola scriptura* person. The only reliable guide to truth was the Bible. That position was later to be re-evaluated in the light of Anglicanism. Tradition and reason had their place too. However, the Bible remained in a position on its own. We do not judge it. It judges us.

In 1958 I was invited by the Rev. John Stott to join the staff of the famous evangelical church in central London, All Souls, Langham Place. It was a great privilege to serve under such a man. He was not a narrow fundamentalist, nor was he a sectarian evangelical. He wanted evangelicals to play a full part in the life of the Anglican Church and also in the wider ecumenical world. He was a strong biblical Christian, who regarded being an evangelical as more important than being an Anglican. I grew up in that atmosphere, in which the Word was more important than the sacraments and being evangelical more important than being an Anglican.

In 1962, my wife and I had a deep experience of the Holy Spirit that changed our lives. It gave us a much deeper love for God and all the things of God. One fruit of this was a new understanding and love for the Bible. That was predictable.

However, what was totally unexpected was a vision of the Church as the Body of Christ and a love for the sacraments, particularly the Eucharist. I was moving towards a wider and more comprehensive understanding of the Christian Faith, which never at any point took me into the liberal camp. I remained deeply committed to the evangelical gospel and the truths revealed in the Scriptures.

We all have our dreams, and I have had my share of them. I don't think I was ever serious about looking for, or ever expected to find, the perfect Church. But my life, like those of many others, has been a voyage of discovery. I have searched for a full-orbed expression of the Christian Faith in the Church.

In the early 1960s I was on retreat in the St. Julian's Community in West Sussex, not far from where we now live. Browsing in the library one morning, I happened to see a book called *The Household of God* by Bishop Lesslie Newbigin (SCM, 1953). I had heard it mentioned several times and recommended by my theological college principal, Dr. (now Bishop) Cyril Bowles. Up to then I had ignored it on the advice of evangelical friends who thought it was "unsound." At that time I was surrounded by a narrow kind of evangelicalism that read only books written by those who believe in the verbal inspiration of the Scriptures. Clearly, as far as they were concerned, this bishop did not pass the test.

One result of my experience of the Holy Spirit was that I was prepared to take a few risks. I hoped these would not damn my soul. So I took the book down and read it. From its pages came a dream, a vision, that has held me firmly ever since. Bishop Newbigin was one of the first theologians to establish the view that the Church is composed of three, not two, spiritualities; to the normal Catholic/Protestant divide needs to be added the "pentecostal." This came as music to my ears and grist to the mill of my mind. It seemed from this that the "pentecostal" experience I had just had was not a random happening. It was the action of the Holy Spirit to bring into focus and reality in my life a vital element that is part of the wholeness of the Church. Thus those who had been swift to condemn pentecostals and the charismatic movement, and to marginalize it, had a defective understanding of this "wholeness."

I then began to see that a true church will be catholic in its life and order, evangelical in its beliefs and mission, and charismatic in its experience and ministry. It seemed a near-perfect scenario. As a committed Anglican, I had high hopes that all this could be seen and become a reality in the life of our church. I am not sure where Bishop Newbigin puts the Orthodox Church—I suppose in the "catholic" category, though that is not where it is at all. In fact, as the Mother Church, it transcends all categories. As I have gone on in my study and experience of Orthodoxy, I have found these three elements wonderfully in equilibrium in the Orthodox Church. I have seen a rich and balanced synthesis of order, sacramental life, biblical authority, mission, and charismatic life.

The Church of England is clearly a mixed church—"comprehensive" is the word used to describe it. Thus I grew up to realize that there were "evangelicals," "Anglo-Catholics," "charismatics," and "modernists," and also others between (like "liberal evangelicals" or "conservative evangelicals"). One of the liberating features of Orthodoxy is that there are virtually no categories like these. This is not to say that there is a common opinion on every issue. I have discovered Orthodox who can think and behave like fundamentalists. Yet there is little or no party spirit; Orthodox will argue theology at the drop of a hat and not mince their words. I have found the whole atmosphere I grew up in of deep division, distrust, and the party mentality to be almost entirely absent.

In the evangelical world everything had to have chapter and verse if it was "true," and evangelism was an imperative that had to be obeyed. I will always be grateful for these two dominant influences in my early life. The problem with evangelicalism is not what it affirms, but what it leaves out. It is these neglected elements which I have increasingly taken on board *without losing the importance of being both biblically and missionary-minded.*

One of the first things I noticed about Orthodoxy was how evangelical it is. I once attended a meeting and heard an Orthodox bishop commenting on the Roman Catholic practice of Benediction (the reverencing of the reserved sacrament). He said, "The gifts are to be consumed, not worshipped." The words might have come from the lips of an evangelical. I soon discovered also that Orthodox people often talk of the "holy table" or the "throne" rather than the "altar."

A major difference between the Orthodox and evangelicals is that Orthodoxy never experienced the Reformation, which gave principal shape to evangelical doctrines and emphases. Sometimes people have asked me, "Do the Orthodox believe in justification by faith?" to which I reply, "Of course. We have always done so." It has never been a controversy in the Orthodox Church. But the Orthodox Church has always had problems with justification by faith *alone (sola fides)* because it contradicts the Scriptures. James writes, "You see then that a man is justified by works, and *not by faith only*" (James 2:24). In the same epistle we read, "Thus also faith by itself, if it does not have works, is dead" (James 2:17). It is God's mercy, not our faith, that saves us, and, "True faith is not just a decision, it's a way of life."[2]

The Eastern Church was largely untouched by other controversies as well, notably those concerning indulgences, relics, the cult of the Virgin Mary, the place of the Scriptures, private masses, and so on. The whole atmosphere of the Reformation is missing in the Orthodox Church. There was no need for such a radical change.

At the end of 1993 a small group of Orthodox priests visited us from the Antiochian Archdiocese of North America. One of them, who stayed with us, was Father Peter Gillquist, the leader of the group of evangelicals who joined the Orthodox Church in 1986. He had been a leader in Campus Crusade for Christ and, as I learned later, a guitar player who likes to play country music. Another priest who stayed with us was Father Bill Olnhausen, a former Episcopalian. He gave us a copy of the book *Coming Home,* which is edited by Father Peter Gillquist (Conciliar Press, 1992); it contains the story of eighteen Protestant ministers in North America who are now priests in the Orthodox Church. They came from such conservative establishments as Campus Crusade for Christ, Oral Roberts University, Westminster Seminary, Asbury Seminary, Bible Baptist College, and Trinity Evangelical Divinity School. They were Baptist, Presbyterian, United Church of Canada, United Methodist, Assemblies of God, and Plymouth Brethren.

Running like a thread through the book is the *quest for the true Church.* One is reminded of the last century when both the Oxford Movement and the Plymouth Brethren, coming from different sides, were wanting "the Church to be the Church," to quote one of the slogans of that period. This was also the quest of some early pioneers of charismatic renewal, which found an expression in what became known as "the house church movement." What John Keble, J. N. Darby, and Arthur Wallis had in view was to find not the perfect Church, but the true Church.

In the authors of the book *Coming Home* one can trace similarities with the early Tractarians. Both groups studied Church history, particularly the Church Fathers. Evangelicals have been notably weak in the study of Church history. Many skip from the days of the Apostles to the Reformers, and everything between is part of the "dark ages" of scriptural error. The evangelicals whose stories are recalled in *Coming Home* were amazed at what they discovered—and it squared with the Scriptures. They found episcopacy, liturgy, tradition, sacraments, and also apostolic truth, all existing *at the time of the Apostles.* And when they looked around to find a Church that had practiced all this since apostolic days, they discovered Orthodoxy.

A Southern Baptist minister called Antony Hughes (now Father Antony) studied Church history. "As a youngster," he writes, "I never dreamed there was anything to predate [my church]. I couldn't even name the preacher who came before Pastor Faulkner, much less the names of any saints or Church Fathers (except Billy Graham and Lottie Moon)! That the Church could be historically traced to Christ and the Apostles was a watershed. There were some in my Church who literally believed that Saint John the Baptist was the founder of the Southern Baptist Convention. . . . From ancient Palestine to colonial Rhode Island was quite a jump!" (*Coming Home,* p. 17).

It would be a mistake to think that it has been easy for these evangelicals to slip into the Orthodox Church. It is not a simple church to join; it has doctrinal and moral standards more stringent than those of some Protestant denominations today. It is not a church that provides an ego trip for those who are dissatisfied with where they are.

But why are so many evangelicals turning to the Orthodox Church? There seems to be among them a sense of incompleteness, a tacit acknowledgment that there are important aspects missing from their own denominations. It has often been pointed out that the Achilles heel of evangelicalism is its failure to take the church seriously. For some their church is just a good boat to fish from; for others it is one that "preaches the gospel."

When the American evangelicals were received into the Orthodox Church, the Patriarch of Antioch, His Beatitude Ignatius IV, wrote this to them (AGAIN magazine, June, 1987):

> In the name of the Holy Synod of Antioch, we bless your glorious work in which we see an unique Antiochian initiative for which the Church is in dire need. This initiative destroys traditional, ethnic, national and cultural barriers. Furthermore, it liberates the Orthodox faith from certain old formalism which froze, confined, victimized, and suffocated the universality of the Orthodox spirit; all that in the name of past history.
>
> Yes, your initiative brings back to the Orthodox faith its universal image. . . . The Orthodox Church is not only for one nation, one civilization and one continent; it is like God, Himself, for all and for every place. . . . [We hope] they [the evangelicals] will inspire us towards a stronger evangelism and a deeper comprehension of the Divine Word.

The Patriarch highlighted the two areas where evangelicals have excelled over the centuries: evangelism and the Bible. He had the grace and humility to welcome them as contributors to, as well as beneficiaries of, Orthodoxy. The evangelicals came home to the Orthodox Church because they saw vital truths to which they had formerly been blinded. They were prepared to come home empty-handed. The Patriarch was wise enough to see that Orthodoxy needed their gifts too. So in the last ten years the Antiochian Patriarchate, especially in North America, has benefited greatly from their inclusion.

When my wife and I first heard about the conversion of so many evangelicals, from such conservative institutions, we marveled. Perhaps we too could make it home to the Orthodox Church without having to denounce all that we had known and experienced before in our lives. Our evangelicalism needed refining, balancing, correcting, readjusting, but it did not need to be cast away as worthless.

We need to look at what lies at the center of evangelical thinking and experience, where it is strongest and weakest at the same time. I am referring to the doctrine of the Church and the relationship between the Scriptures and Tradition.

1 *Becoming Orthodox,* Conciliar Press, 1989, p. 4.

2 In the section on "Justification by Faith" in the Orthodox Study Bible (Thomas Nelson, 1993), p. 348. This study Bible is based on the New King James Version, and its notes are strongly influenced by the evangelical influence in the Orthodox Church in the United States. It makes fascinating reading.

14

Church, the Scriptures, and Tradition

Liturgy, sacrament, episcopal government did not necessarily come easily. . . . That they were true and everywhere in the ancient Church was for us regrettably obvious. We had no argument there. The tough thing about early Christianity for us came in doing *it.*

Peter Gillquist [1]

When I was a student at theological college in Cambridge, I remember heated discussions about the nature of the Church. In those days one had to defend Anglicanism against the attacks of fellow evangelicals from other denominations. These ranged from the Plymouth Brethren to the Baptists, who believed in the "gathered church," centered on the Bible and containing no "nominal Christians." One of the key questions we Anglicans were asked was, "What would you do if the Church of England became unitarian (or heretical in another way)?" As a new convert, I found this question quite daunting. However, my friends, who had been longer in the faith than I, had a stock argument: "Parliament would never agree to it."

In the 1950s and 1960s so-called "Erastianism" (the idea that the state has the right to exercise jurisdiction in ecclesiastical matters) was still strong, though it was on the way out. I remember being bemused by the suggestion that our church had to rely on a secular Parliament to defend the faith. Parliament was not then, any more than it is now, renowned for its Christian character. The more I went on, the more dissatisfied

I became with evangelical teaching about the Church. Then in 1962 I had my charismatic experience. Among other things this was to change for ever my view of the Church. It opened many doors in my mind, the most important of which was to lead to the Orthodox Church.

This new view of the Church has colored all my experience as a "charismatic." In the early 1960s a booklet by Larry Christenson, *Speaking in Tongues: A Gift for the Body of Christ,* proved popular in Britain. When I followed it up with a booklet on prophecy, I called it *Prophecy: A Gift for the Body of Christ.* I saw instinctively that the gifts of the Holy Spirit are given primarily for the Church, not for the individual. The fact that those who manifest the gifts are blessed too is secondary. And the gifts of the Holy Spirit need to be accepted humbly, not with pride or a sense of achievement.

When I was writing this book, I went through some old papers. I found an article I had written in a newsletter called *Work and Worship,* dated October, 1963. It was written during my time at All Souls Church, Langham Place, a year or so after I had my fresh vision of the Church as the Body of Christ. The article was called, "What Is Wrong with the Church?" After a section on "revival and reformation," I turned to "the doctrine of the Church" and "organism or organization?" I wrote, "There is a need for a re-examination of the biblical doctrine of the Church. The Church is God's living temple on earth, where the Holy Spirit dwells and Christ is represented. There must not only be a cleansing of the temple, but a rediscovery of what the temple really is." *A major problem today is that people have become so taken up with "cleansing" or "empowering" that they have ceased to consider a more primary question, "What is the Church?"*

I suppose I had rather naïvely assumed that all my fellow charismatics believed the same. I was increasingly to see that this was not so; and in the 1980s and 1990s the focus has shifted more and more to individual blessings. The gifts have become more isolated from the Church, largely through an increasing emphasis on "signs and wonders."

Sacraments and Authority

When all this began to happen to me in the 1960s, one of the first fruits was a new awareness of the crucial place the sacraments have. This was especially true of what Anglicans call Holy Communion. I also saw the importance of the traditional services and the old prayers and liturgies. At the first charismatic conference I ever organized, held at Stoke Poges Manor House, the Holy Communion service lasted all day! I deliberately kept the old service but allowed the gifts of the Spirit and other spontaneous contributions to fit into the liturgical framework.

I was fortified by the words of Jesus Christ, "Therefore every scribe instructed concerning the kingdom of heaven is like a householder who brings out of his treasure things new and old" (Matthew 13:52). Increasingly I have seen Christians ignoring the old, even despising it. This has led to a devaluing of the sacraments. The main focus of church life has ceased to be (as it was from earliest times) the Eucharist.

Throughout the 1970s and 1980s I experienced considerable exposure to the charismatic renewal in the Roman Catholic Church. For me it witnessed to the reality of the point I have just been making. Here were men and women expressing a glorious freedom in Christ, with the full flow of the charisms of the Holy Spirit, yet also integrating the whole thing in the sacraments, which were still highly honored. They also respected the authority structure of the Church.

Much credit for this must go to Cardinal Suenens, who took a great deal of trouble to find out for himself what the charismatic renewal was all about; he came to the conclusion that it was in keeping with both the Scriptures and the traditions of the Roman Catholic Church. So he committed himself wholly to it while also working towards the goal of bringing it to the heart of the Roman Catholic Church. Sadly, Protestant churches of Europe and North America had few champions of the charismatic renewal. We were fortunate in the Anglican Church to have leaders like the former Bishop of Singapore, Chiu Ban It, and the late Archbishop of Cape Town and Primate of South Africa, Bill Burnett.

So from 1962 onwards I was serious about the Church, its sacraments, its authority, and its continuity in history. Of course, I soon found out that all four are central to the life of the Orthodox Church, and, in fact, are fully realized nowhere else.

Are Bishops Necessary?

As an evangelical I had for a long time regarded the position of the bishop in the Church as ambiguous. I suppose I settled down, as many do, in a middle position. I could not accept the bishop as necessary for the Church; on the other hand, I did not see him as an optional extra, the equivalent of a moderator in the Presbyterian Church or a chairman in the Methodist Church.[2] Gradually, however, my position changed, particularly as I observed how bishops operated in the Roman Catholic Church and, later, the Orthodox Church.

As I have already pointed out, the Orthodox Church believes in the principle of *primus inter pares* or "first among equals." Orthodox bishops do rule in the Church, but they do so collegially with their fellow bishops. Even the Ecumenical Patriarch is first among equals—and woe betide him if he tries to assume papal powers! So we need to look carefully at the principle of *episcope,* which has been controversial since the Reformation. The question is: Are bishops of the *esse* of the Church or the *bene esse?* Or, putting it more simply, are bishops essential, or are they just one good idea among several?

The most helpful book I have read on this subject was written by a former Archbishop of Canterbury, the late Michael Ramsey. He wrote it in 1936, when he was comparatively young, and it is called *The Gospel and the Catholic Church* (Longman, 1936). In this book the author quotes F. D. Maurice, who said, "The task of a theologian is to dig rather than to build" (p. 221). Michael Ramsey goes on to say that we have to dig in the fields of Christian origins and Church history. He continues, "The digging discloses not only lessons but the fact of the divine foundation, for as the débris of old controversies and one-sided systems is cleared away, there appears the pattern of a structure, whose maker and builder is God" (p. 222).

If we look at the history of the Church from the first century to its break-up at the Reformation, we see unmistakably that the episcopate is the organ of continuity and unity. It still is today in the Orthodox and Roman Catholic churches. What came as revelation to me was the fact that *this teaching was there in the very first generation of the Church. It was not challenged until many centuries later.*

One vital person I "discovered" during my pilgrimage to the Orthodox Church was Saint Ignatius of Antioch. I had known something about him before, in the days when theological students studied Church history. Here was a man who lived at the same time as the Apostle John. He was not only a bishop himself, without contradiction, but also one who believed in episcopacy. Then, and during the following centuries, there was never a hint that there was a wide choice of types of leadership from which you could take your pick. It was bishops or the independent sects.

Saint Ignatius makes this abundantly clear, and no one ever challenged him in the coming centuries. He wrote, "Let no man do anything about matters concerning the Church without the bishop" (*Smyrn.* 8). And "Let that be held a valid Eucharist which is under the bishop or to whom he shall have committed it." That principle is upheld by the Orthodox Church to this day. Later Saint Irenaeus wrote, "We can give the names of the bishops *whom the apostles appointed* in the several churches, with the list of their successors from that day to this" (*Adv. Haer.*, III, iii, 6).

Michael Ramsey, in summarizing the evidence, writes, "Episcopacy was universal by the second half of the second century." He goes on, "There is no trace of opposition to this growth, and there was even a belief that the apostles had ordered it" (*The Gospel and the Catholic Church,* p. 77).

History here is on the side of the Orthodox Church. The only people to question the universal acceptance of episcopacy, as of the very essence of the Church, were the heretics and the sectarians, who either denied the apostolic faith or rebelled against the apostolic order.

Scripture and Tradition

Evangelicals, when examining anything, will always ask the question, "Is it scriptural?" Some argue that we are to do nothing and believe nothing that is not explicitly stated in the Bible. Others see the issue differently: we are to do nothing and believe nothing that is contrary to the Scriptures. Sooner or later the matter of tradition emerges, because the Orthodox believe in the authority of the Scriptures *and* that of Holy Tradition. This needs some explanation.

For the Orthodox the Scriptures *are* Holy Tradition—the most highly regarded and honored element of it. But there is other Holy Tradition that Orthodox believe. For example, the first seven Ecumenical Councils, though not part of the Scriptures, are certainly regarded as part of what the Church believes and are wholly scriptural. Again, the Holy Trinity is never mentioned explicitly in the Scriptures, although it is implicit throughout,[3] even in the Old Testament. The word "Trinity" is entirely absent, yet belief in the Trinity is crucial to the faith of the Orthodox.

On the issue of tradition, some evangelical Bible translators are not consistent in their translation of the word, and it is not unreasonable to suspect a hidden agenda. When the word is used in a bad sense, it is translated "tradition." But when the same Greek word is used positively, it is sometimes translated as "teachings," as, for example, in 2 Thessalonians 2:15.

The word is used negatively, for example, in Matthew 15:3–6 when Jesus says, "Why do you also transgress the commandment of God because of your tradition?. . . you have made the commandment of God of no effect by your tradition." Saint Paul also refers negatively to it in Colossians 2:8, "Beware lest anyone cheat you through philosophy and empty deceit, according to the tradition of men, according to the basic principles of the world, and not according to Christ."

We should note that Jesus refers to "*your* tradition" (in other words, human and not divine) and Saint Paul to "the tradition of men" based on the principles of the world. The world has its traditions, but those do not rule out the traditions of God. For in 2 Thessalonians Saint Paul writes, "Therefore, brethren, stand fast and hold the traditions which you were taught, whether by word or our epistle" (2 Thess. 2:15), and later, "But we command you, brethren, in the name of our Lord Jesus Christ, that you withdraw from every brother who walks disorderly and not according to the tradition which he received from us" (2 Thess. 3:6). In both these passages, the New International Version uses the word "teaching" instead of "tradition." The Orthodox are consistent and believe that the Scriptures are "tradition," just as the Ecumenical Councils and creeds are. And all are part of the holy teaching of the Church.

One of the most important Scriptures in relation to this point is 1 Timothy 3:15. Saint Paul writes about the Church as "the house of God, which is the church of the living God, *the pillar and ground of the truth.*" He does not say that the Bible is the ground of the truth, but that the Church is. The words, "the Bible says . . ." need to be balanced by the words, "the Church says . . ." We need to add, "The Bible says that the Church has a right to say . . ." The Church is called to guard the good deposit of the truth entrusted to it. The place of the Church needs always to balance that of the Scriptures. They have different functions, but they belong together. The slogan *sola scriptura* is not sufficient. On its own it has led to the proliferation of denominations, each claiming to be faithful to the truth.

Calling Priests "Father"

When I was first in touch with the Orthodox in earnest, as an Anglican priest, I was invariably called "father." Since becoming an Orthodox priest, I have been called nothing else. I believe it is one of the strengths of Orthodoxy. Some have found it difficult to accept. The Scripture that is frequently quoted against the practice is Matthew 23:9: "Do not call anyone on earth your father; for One is your Father, He who is in heaven." To interpret this literally, and out of its context, makes a nonsense of it. Since the injunction is "do not call *anyone* on earth your father," it would rule out children calling their parent "Father" or "Daddy."

We observe that Saint Paul refers to Timothy as his "son," so presumably the apostle was Timothy's "father." In 1 Timothy 1:2 Saint Paul calls Timothy "a true son in the faith" (see also 2 Timothy 1:2 and 2:1). Today in the Western world there is a crying need for the restoration of fatherhood in the family. The modern campaign against the patriarchal element in family life is deeply harmful. In the Scriptures the human family and the divine family (the Church) are closely related. We need more, not less, of the patriarchal element in both Church and family.

What, then, is Jesus prohibiting? It is surely the making of men into gods by giving them divine titles and treating them in this way. That was the weakness of the Pharisees who, through human pride, seized for themselves titles like "rabbi," "teacher," and "father." In the Orthodox world we use titles like "father" or "master" (for the bishop) out of respect and to express a human relationship, not to ascribe divinity to their owners.

Names

One interesting aspect of this topic is the importance that the Orthodox Church attaches to names. This is one instance in which the Orthodox are more sensitive to the Scriptures than many evangelicals. You must have a name which is truly Christian, and if you are received into the Church without one, you will be given one at your baptism or reception and chrismation. Some time ago we witnessed the baptism and reception of a young Muslim woman in an Orthodox church. Her sponsor chose her name and gave it to her at the service. It was the name of a saint of the Church who was being commemorated on that day.

On a visit to the Middle East in 1995 my wife and I visited a restaurant in Damascus. Our waiter introduced himself with the words, "My name is George," which was his way of saying, "I am a Christian." When we arrived at Beirut airport on the same visit, the immigration official discussed my name. The immigration form required my father's Christian name and so on. On our way home another immigration officer saw my name. "My name also is Michael," he said, expressing great interest. "It means 'who is like unto God'," I said to him. I can't imagine a British official taking the slightest interest in anyone's name, even his own.

Confidence in Orthodoxy

It is my view that evangelicals can find their home in the Orthodox Church. Of course, adjustments are necessary. However, one can have a great deal more confidence in a Church that has stood the test of nearly two thousand years than in a comparative newcomer to the scene like evangelicalism.

It is worth noting that some of the major figures in the move to Rome by Tractarians in the nineteenth century were those who had grown up in the evangelical wing of the Church of England. This is true of the two who became cardinals, John Henry Newman and Henry Manning, and of the two sons of the famous philanthropist William Wilberforce, Henry (received in 1850) and Robert (received in 1854).

There is another compelling reason for confidence in the Orthodox Church. Apart from its age, there is its unity. There have been, and still are, many quarrels and what politicians euphemistically call "local difficulties." However, with the exception of the split with the Oriental Orthodox in the fifth century, which is now happily on the way to being reconciled, the Orthodox Church has remained largely united in communion with itself. Evangelicalism, on the other hand, has split into thousands of denominations holding a whole range of beliefs that sometimes bear little relationship to true orthodoxy. Evangelicals can have complete confidence in the Orthodox Church, not just for themselves, but for their children and their children's children.

1 *Becoming Orthodox,* p. 47.

2 In the U.K. Methodists have chairmen instead of bishops.

3 Two of the most important feasts in the Orthodox Church are the Holy Theophany (January 6) and the Holy Transfiguration (August 6). Both are seen as Trinitarian events in the life of Christ; the Theophany commemorates not, as in the West, the coming of the wise men to Christ, but Christ's baptism in the Jordan, when the voice of the Father is heard and the Holy Spirit comes on Christ. At the Transfiguration the voice of the Father is again heard, and the cloud from heaven is believed to represent the coming of the Holy Spirit, as in the reference to the Annunciation (Luke 1:35), when it was said, "The power of the Most High will overshadow you."

15

Is the Orthodox Church Charismatic?

We must never dissociate the institutional Church from the charismatic Church. They are but two aspects of the same reality.

Cardinal Leon Joseph Suenens

The late Cardinal Suenens was among the most influential church leaders of the twentieth century. He was one of the architects of the Second Vatican Council and so was crucially involved in the renewal of the structures of the Roman Catholic Church, and, as I have mentioned, he was a strong supporter and encourager of the charismatic renewal. In a letter to Pope Paul VI (July 24, 1973), he wrote, "It is my opinion that the charismatics represent one of the most powerful graces of renewal in today's Church." He never regarded the charismatic movement and the doctrine and authority of the Church as mutually exclusive. Both have their place. To use his own words, both are "aspects of the same reality." In other words, both are gifts of God; each is important and needs the other.

Sadly, not all church leaders have had the courage and spiritual balance of Cardinal Suenens. The tendency has been for conflict between the two to arise and for schisms to follow. We should not be surprised by this because the problem surfaced in the earliest period of the life of the Christian Church. It had to be faced by the Apostles themselves, particularly, though not exclusively, by Saint Paul. The church in Corinth had many problems, and clearly it was excessive in its charismatic experiences. Those whom the Apostle mockingly called the "most eminent apostles" ("superstars") were in charge (2 Cor. 11:5). These men criticized Saint Paul for not being charismatic enough.

In his response Saint Paul did not proscribe the charismatic manifestations; actually, he encouraged them: "Pursue love, and desire spiritual gifts, but especially that you may prophesy" (1 Cor. 14:1). He also encouraged the Corinthians to speak in tongues: "I wish you all spoke with tongues" (1 Cor. 14:5). His approach was to balance the gifts of the Holy Spirit with order in the Church, which included the assertion of his apostolic authority. The gifts were to be manifested in an orderly fashion. Individualism was not to be encouraged; everything was to be done "for the profit of all" (1 Cor. 12:7). Services were to be conducted "decently and in order" (1 Cor. 14:40). The overarching criterion had to be, "Does this edify (build up) the Church?" (1 Cor. 14:12, 26, 31). The Church down the centuries, from the Montanists onwards, has had to face similar tensions.

One of the questions I am most frequently asked is, "Is there a charismatic renewal in the Orthodox Church?" The quickest and easiest response is, "No, the Orthodox Church *is* charismatic." That is too simple an answer, however; we need to explore the matter more deeply.

The Person of the Holy Spirit

The Orthodox Church has always honored the Holy Spirit as a Person of the Holy Trinity, truly God. The importance of the Holy Spirit was stressed by the Church Fathers. Saint Athanasius wrote, "The Word took flesh, that we might receive the Spirit." Bishop Kallistos Ware comments, "From one point of view, the whole 'aim' of the Incarnation is the sending of the Spirit at Pentecost" (*The Orthodox Church,* p. 230).

This was clearly proclaimed by Saint Peter at Pentecost. He

told the crowd, "Repent, and let every one of you be baptized in the name of Jesus Christ for the remission of sins; *and you shall receive the gift of the Holy Spirit"* (Acts 2:38). Saint Seraphim of Sarov, in his famous conversation with Nikolai Motovilov, said, "The true aim of the Christian life is the acquisition of the Holy Spirit of God." Vladimir Lossky comments, "This may at first sight appear oversimplified, but it does sum up the whole spiritual tradition of the Orthodox Church."[1]

The basis of the Orthodox Church's consistent witness to the Holy Spirit, compared with His neglect by the Western Church, lies in its adherence to the original wording of the Nicene Creed. The controversy over the *filioque* clause, which was added to the Nicene Creed by the Western church and was, as we have seen, a major factor in precipitating the Great Schism, was not a quibble over words. It had deep and lasting consequences in the life of the Church.

To say that the Spirit proceeds from the Father, as the Son is begotten by the Father, places the three Persons of the Trinity in a balanced triangle, with the Father as the Head and all three Persons of equal value and importance. To say that the Spirit proceeds from the Father *and the Son,* on the other hand, tends to reduce the Spirit to a position subordinate to the other two. He becomes a sort of "effluvium" emanating from the relationship of Father and Son, rather than a Person in His own right. The charismatic movement, perceiving this wrongful devaluing of the Spirit in the Western tradition but too far divorced from Orthodox Tradition to understand its cause, has in some cases overreacted by elevating Him to the first place in the life of the Church, to the detriment of the Father and the Son.

The Holy Spirit and Baptism

Some charismatic scholars, however, have attempted to go back to the early witness of the Church to ground their view of the Holy Spirit. One example of this is the book, *Christian Initiation and Baptism in the Holy Spirit* (The Liturgical Press, 1991), written by two Roman Catholic scholars, Kilian McDonnell and George Montague. George Montague does the biblical studies, and Kilian McDonnell contributes studies of some of the Church Fathers. It is interesting that he selects a number of Eastern Church Fathers, including Cyril of Jerusalem, Philoxenus (from the Syrian Jacobite tradition), and John Chrysostom. He thus shows the richness of the Eastern Orthodox spiritual life and the way it has so clearly honored the Holy Spirit of God.

I will attempt to summarize this carefully argued and researched book. Its main thesis is that Christian initiation was from the beginning modeled on the baptism of Jesus or on his death and Resurrection, and involved essentially the gift of the Holy Spirit; also that the charisms of the Spirit, though not the central reality, were clearly considered "an integral element of that central reality that was the gift of the Spirit." [2] This baptism in the Holy Spirit was also an experience. The Church Fathers were not afraid to call it that, as Saint Symeon the New Theologian testifies. Kilian McDonnell writes, "If by experience we mean not mere feelings but an effect that transforms and empowers lives, then clearly the earliest Christian initiation was an experience."[3] Regrettably, both the focus on Christ's baptism and the link with charisms were lost in time. Perhaps the time has come for their recovery.

There is not enough space here to go into the teaching of the Church Fathers. They consistently upheld the gift of the Holy Spirit as a crucial factor in Christian initiation. The Eastern Church has always seen the importance of the baptism of Christ by John in the River Jordan. It sees it as a Trinitarian experience—the voice of the Father to the Son and the coming of the Holy Spirit as a dove upon Him. Many Church Fathers, especially the earlier ones, saw the baptism of Christ (with the coming of the Holy Spirit) as the model of Christian baptism.

The Orthodox Church still emphasizes the importance of this in the Feast of the Holy Theophany, which is centered on Christ's baptism. The spread of the heresy of adoptionism, which usually regarded Christ's baptism as the moment of his becoming the Son of God, saw the reduction of Christ's baptism as a model in the West. It became less and less the model for our own baptism and was replaced by Paul's teaching in Romans 6 of baptismal death and resurrection. This meant that the gift of the Holy Spirit, as an integral part of baptism, tended to be neglected, and the focus shifted to Christ's death and Resurrection.

The Orthodox Church does not, as we shall see, exclude the idea of further experiences of the Holy Spirit after the initiation of water baptism and chrismation. Father Lev Gillet writes:

> The gift of the Holy Spirit cannot be exclusively identified with Charisma . . . in many modern cases we should not dare to deny the reality of a "baptism of the Spirit" conferred upon men who had not received it sacramentally . . . the grace of the Holy Spirit is already active in the baptism with water as well as the grace of the Father and the grace of the Son. But there is a special sending of the Spirit to man; and a baptism in water not completed by the baptism with the Holy Ghost would manifest a deficient Christian life . . . the question of Paul to the Ephesian disciples, "Did ye receive the Holy Spirit . . . ?" [Acts 19:2] is asked of every one of us. It would not be enough to answer, "I have received the mystery or sacrament of the Spirit after my baptism, when I was anointed with the Holy Chrism."[4]

The Holy Spirit and the Liturgy

The way the Orthodox Church has honored the Holy Spirit is reflected clearly in the Divine Liturgy. The Orthodox Church has faithfully kept the *Epiclesis* (the invocation of the Holy Spirit on the people and the Gifts) in the Liturgy, and this is respected by other churches.[5] Some revised liturgies of these churches now include it. The Church of England, for example, has a form of Epiclesis in the first and third eucharistic prayers in the *Alternative Service Book.* Yet only in the third is the invocation of the Holy Spirit on the people, and here it occurs after the prayer of consecration itself. When it occurs in the consecration prayer, then it invokes the power, not the Person, of the Holy Spirit, as in the Orthodox Liturgy.

The Epiclesis comes at the center point of the Divine Liturgy, during the *Anaphora* (elevation of the Gifts). The priest says, "Send down thy Holy Spirit *upon us* and upon these gifts here spread forth." Thus the priest asks the Holy Spirit to transform the worshippers as well as changing the bread and the wine into the body and blood of Christ. Father Lev Gillet writes about this moment:

> Even in the context of the eucharistic liturgy, the Spirit is not given only for the sake of the Eucharist itself. The purpose of his coming is to lead us into "Pentecostal life," the life of the Spirit. Have we ever taken seriously the promises of the Lord Jesus after his resurrection, made not only to his apostles but to every believer? Have we ever believed that, in the name of Jesus, we are able to exorcise demons and heal the sick? The Lord Jesus himself declared it to be true. It represents a sad lack of trust when we do not even dare try to exercise (with faith, humility and submission to the divine will) the powers which Christ has invested in his faithful ones

> . . . have the Savior's evangelical promises been made in vain?[6]

There are other moments in the Liturgy when the Holy Spirit is invoked. There is the opening prayer, "O heavenly King, Comforter, the Spirit of Truth . . . come and abide in us." Priests who are concelebrating greet each other and say, "May the Holy Spirit descend upon you and the power of the Most High overshadow you." At that most holy moment when the priest places the Lamb (the consecrated bread) in the chalice, he says, "The fullness [of the cup of faith] of the Holy Spirit." When the warm water is blessed and added, the priest says, "The warmth of faith full of the Holy Spirit."

In Orthodoxy an important place is given to the work of the Holy Spirit in and through the lives of Christians, not only the saints but also ordinary people. The word often used to describe it is "deification." According to Saint Athanasius, God became man *that we might become god.* Saint Peter states boldly in 2 Peter 1:3, 4: "His divine power has given to us all things that pertain to life and godliness, through the knowledge of Him who called us by glory and virtue, by which have been given to us exceedingly great and precious promises, that through these *you may be partakers of the divine nature,* having escaped the corruption that is in the world through lust."

The Gifts of the Holy Spirit

We have seen already that the Orthodox Church was hardly touched by the Reformation. So the issues of faith, order, and thought that rocked Europe during the fifteenth and sixteenth centuries largely passed the Orthodox Church by. It is also true to say that the so-called Enlightenment, which has been perhaps the major fashioner of European thought and life from the Renaissance to Marxist Communism, affected the Eastern

Church only marginally. There were points of contact and attempts by some to Westernize the Orthodox Church, but on the whole the two churches of East and West functioned quite separately. We sometimes refer to our age as "post-modern." The Age of Enlightenment is now called "modernity." In that case, the Orthodox Church is pre-modern. It has been little influenced by the huge groundswell of this modernity.

One aspect of the Reformation was the clash of two currents of thought—the mystical and the rationalistic. Already people were saying, "Christians can't believe in that," meaning perhaps miraculous signs pushed to the limit by a superstitious and uneducated populace and an increasingly corrupt church. The Reformers quite rightly saw false elements in much of the search for miracles in the Middle Ages but, sadly, threw the baby out with the bath water. They failed to follow the pattern of the Apostle Paul, who advocated proper use of charisms, not non-use, as the answer to the false.

The Reformation sowed the seeds of the whole "modern" movement that has increasingly opposed supernaturalism—in the end, even the Virgin Birth and the bodily Resurrection of Christ. Fortunately, the Orthodox Church never had the Enlightenment to undermine its confidence in God who, through the Incarnation, has invaded human life and the whole physical world in a new way. Also the Church has always believed in the presence and power of the Holy Spirit. It has always trusted in the continuing presence of that Spirit. The Orthodox Church sees the Holy Spirit at work in the Church, expressly in the forming of Holy Tradition, which is a sign of the constant presence of the Holy Spirit guiding us "into all truth" (John 16:13), and in the lives of church people doing miracles and manifesting His power. Most of its saints have performed miracles to the glory of God and the blessing of the Church and the world.

Many waves have battered Protestantism. One of them has been called "dispensationalism." This denies the operation of charisms after the death of the last Apostle; so all miracles today are questionable. This wave has hardly caused a ripple in Orthodoxy. As a Church it has never questioned the presence of the gifts of the Spirit. It has also rightly seen the importance of proper discernment as to the source of power and the need to sanctify the human element in the presentation of these gifts to the Church and the world.

Orthodox teachers do not carve up time into convenient "dispensations." We are in the Christian era, in which Christ was manifested in the flesh and the Holy Spirit given to the Church that He might glorify Christ. The Spirit of God continues through the Church to manifest the signs and wonders that undoubtedly accompanied the Apostles and their disciples. The Orthodox Church is often accused of being in a time warp. Nonsense! It is some Protestants who have invented time warps to suit their theological predilections. The Orthodox Church has always accepted the gifts of the Holy Spirit in the life of the Church. Father Lev Gillet writes:

> The gifts of the Spirit, which marked the beginnings of the Church are not things of the past. They have been given, they *are* given, to the Church for all times . . . only their lack of faith inclines contemporary Christians to consider charismatic manifestations in our days exceptional. If they are exceptional it is because of a lack of faith similar to that which hindered Jesus at Nazareth (Matthew 13:58). But the power of the Holy Spirit is as alive today as it was in the days of the Book of Acts. The mighty works accomplished then in the name of Jesus . . . can be accomplished now, if only we had faith (Mark 16:17, 18). (*Orthodox Spirituality*, pp. 69, 72)

It is important for us to grasp this. It is not for us to look back on the Acts of the Apostles only with nostalgia. The same Holy Spirit is actively present in the Church today. As Lev Gillet writes, "The saints are the heirs and successors of the 'charismatics' of the first centuries" (*Orthodox Spirituality*, p. 71).

Discernment

For all Christians, discernment (which Saint Paul lists as one of the gifts of the Holy Spirit) is particularly important when it comes to the charisms of the Holy Spirit. Power can be dangerous, but the power *(dunamis)* of the Holy Spirit was promised and received by the whole Church, Apostles and laity alike, at Pentecost. For the Orthodox two considerations are paramount: first, ensuring that all things conform to the teaching of the Church in the Scriptures and the rest of Holy Tradition; and, second, proper order and submission within the Church, particularly to one's bishop. The Church needs to be safeguarded against maverick operators and the individualism which marks, and mars, so much of our Western life.

The Orthodox Church has always had a keen awareness of the attacks of Satan and evil spirits. The battle with satanic power is a constant refrain in the lives of monastics and of ordinary men and women in the Church. As in the Roman Catholic Church, the Orthodox have an important place in the baptism service for the renouncing of Satan, even spitting on him! Exorcism has a place in the life of the Church, but with proper safeguards. Saint Cyril of Jerusalem writes, "Divine exorcisms, borrowed from the Scripture, purify the soul." The powers of darkness are an important factor in our spiritual fight. We should be careful not to overlook the reality and the strength of objective evil.

From earliest times the Church has had to struggle with the

question of discerning individual spiritual experiences and how to evaluate them. The Montanist movement challenged the Church in the second century, and one of the ablest theologians of that time, Tertullian, joined them. The conversion of Tertullian to this strongly charismatic community should make us take the subject seriously, for Tertullian was no mean theologian.

The Orthodox Church has often had to face the tension between Church structures and Church order on the one hand, and experiences of the Holy Spirit on the other. In chapter 11 we looked at the icon controversy that rocked the Eastern Church to its foundations. It needed an Ecumenical Council to settle the matter. Similar struggles have taken place over the issue of charismatic grace over against the hierarchy and the ordering of the Church; individual experiences as opposed to the corporate life of the Church; apostolic order compared with, and sometimes in conflict with, apostolic life. The acceptance of experiences of the Holy Spirit in the Church goes back to the Apostles and the Church Fathers, particularly Saint Basil the Great.

Two men stand out in this area of controversy. The first was Saint Symeon (949–1022), called the New Theologian, and the other Saint Gregory Palamas (c. 1296–1359). Let us look at them in turn.

Saint Symeon

Saint Symeon was named by the Church the "New Theologian." This gave him recognition alongside two others similarly called "Theologian," Saint Gregory of Nazianzus (329–389) and Saint John the Evangelist. Saint Symeon was born in Galatea in Asia Minor. He was from a noble background and came under the influence of his spiritual father, Saint Symeon the Studite, at the monastery of Stoudion in Constantinople.

He later moved to the monastery of Saint Mamas, where he became a monk and, later, abbot.[7]

Saint Symeon was one of the most outstanding of all Orthodox mystics. He stressed the importance of personal repentance, the gift of tears, and the personal reception of the Holy Spirit. He stood for the revival of the spiritual life at a time when, even in the monasteries, the prayer life and morals of Christian people were lax. This great theologian and monk also stressed what the Orthodox call "deification," or sharing in the divine nature through grace. He taught that this was the crown of spiritual endeavor. He was probably the father of the so-called Hesychast movement (the Greek word means "quiet"). This is closely associated with the "Jesus Prayer" and is still a strong force in Orthodoxy. The movement was nurtured on Mount Athos, the Holy Mountain. Saint Symeon is also the author of several prayers to the Holy Spirit, which are comparatively rare in the Orthodox Church. He witnessed the tragic separation of theology from experience. Thus worship became formal and faith nominal. He felt responsible to recall the Church to authentic Christian experience and called himself the "enthusiastic zealot."

Saint Symeon believed that all the people of God could have intimacy with, and experience of, Christ through the Holy Spirit. He taught that this was as important as hierarchical authority, and his views brought him into conflict with the hierarchy of his day, especially Archbishop Stephan. He challenged, as charismatics do today, formalism and conventionality. His teaching revolved around spiritual exercises such as prayer, fasting, penitence (especially with tears), and the partaking of the Holy Spirit. He used to refer to a "second baptism" (as Pentecostals and charismatics do today), which gave Christians a deeper conversion and consciousness of Christ.

Saint Gregory Palamas

Saint Gregory Palamas went to Mount Athos as a monk in 1318. It was there that he came under the influence of the Hesychasts, whose teaching and practices he was later to defend. The climax of the controversy he encountered was open conflict between Saint Gregory and a Calabrian monk, Barlaam, who had been strongly influenced by Western theology. The Hesychasts claimed the spiritual experience of seeing the "divine light." Barlaam and others denied the possibility of such an experience because no person can see God. Saint Gregory distinguished between the divine "essence," which no one can see, and the divine "energy," which can be seen. In 1351 the Blachernae Synod recognized the orthodoxy of Saint Gregory's teaching.

These great theologians never allowed mystical experiences to replace the Holy Sacraments or the divine order of the Church. The full recovery of the power and graces of Pentecost is important for the life of the Orthodox Church, as for other churches. And God has provided the safeguard for this in Holy Tradition and the episcopal structures of the Church.

There has been a need in Orthodoxy for constant vigilance against those who have wanted to suppress the charisms of the Spirit and other experiences of God—in Western parlance, "mysticism." Martyrs like Ignatius of Antioch, Felicitas and Perpetua, and many others witnessed to the spiritual Christ. They knew the actual charismatic presence of the Lord as the great fact behind the whole Christian movement. Lev Gillet asks the question, "Do we believe as intensely in the reality of the spiritual Christ?" He goes on to say, "For us the danger is of localizing and limiting the Pentecostal Christ within the Apostolic times, and so failing to acknowledge he is *just as much present* now as he was then" (*Orthodox Spirituality,* p. 80).

Let us now look at one incident in the life of Saint Innocent, the "Enlightener"[8] of the people of the Aleutian Islands.

A Saintly Example

We have seen that the Orthodox Church is not opposed to charismatic gifts or baptism in the Holy Spirit. Indeed, as we have shown, its liturgies and sacraments are more expressive of them than those of the Western churches. Yet it is opposed to the way they are sometimes manifested, and it rightly questions from time to time the reality of some claims.

A good example of the Orthodox approach can be seen in the life of Saint Innocent of Alaska. He evangelized the Aleutian Islands and, later, Alaska from his native Russia. The work he did in the Aleutians could hardly have been done under more trying circumstances. The weather was often dangerously stormy, and he had to travel from island to island in a simple kayak. On one occasion he was visiting one of the new churches and hearing confessions. One of those confessing was an old man called Smirennikov, who was alleged to be a shaman or seer. On the previous day he had prophesied, "A priest will come today. He is already on his way, and he'll teach you to pray to God." He even described Saint Innocent's appearance. The man had been known to heal people miraculously, and there were many stories of his charismatic gifts.

Father John (Saint Innocent) talked with the man, and he was amazed by the extent of his knowledge of the gospel. He also discovered that he could neither read nor write. When he asked him bluntly how he had learned all this, Smirennikov replied that two companions had taught him. Intrigued by this answer, Father John asked who they were. "White men," the old man replied, and then described what they had told him.

Father John asked where they were and was told they lived nearby in the mountains. "They visit me every day," the old man said. When he described their appearance, it tallied with the way in which the Archangel Gabriel is portrayed on icons. Apparently for over thirty years they appeared to him almost every day, in daylight or in the early evening, never at night.

In his report Father John told his bishop that these angelic beings had taught the man Christian theology in its totality and the mysteries of the faith. "Their doctrine is that of the Orthodox faith," he wrote. They even taught him how to pray and how to behave in his marriage. The old man offered to take Father John to meet them. Father John hesitated. He wrote to the bishop: "I am filled with fear and humility . . . I am unworthy; I'd best not go. I have been convinced that the spirits which appear to this old man (if indeed they do appear) are not devils, for although the devil can indeed at times transform himself into an angel of light, he never does so for purposes of exhortation and salvation but always for the destruction of man . . ."[9]

Archbishop Michael of Urkutsk gave his blessing for Father John to visit the angels, but it was not to be. By the time the bishop's reply reached him, John Smirennikov had died peacefully, having foretold the day and the hour of his passing.

When I read this story, I was struck by the obedience of this priest, his humility, his awareness of the awesomeness of God and His angels. Had he been a modern charismatic, not a few books would have been written about it in the next six months. Trips by jet would have been quickly arranged to visit the "Aleutian Blessing." The Orthodox Church isn't like that, although it too has had experience of the charisms of the Spirit. The Orthodox Church does not encourage individualism. It was proper for Father John to ask his bishop to bless him and to do nothing until he had. It was typical too of the saints of Orthodoxy that the man refused to publicize what had happened or to make money or gain popularity and success through it.

At the back of this is the awareness that when this sort of thing happens you should not be surprised. It is part of the normal life of the Church, so why speak so extravagantly about it? As Lev Gillet writes: "We should not feel reluctant to acknowledge direct divine interventions, which break the so-called natural laws . . . saints and charismatics are the liberators of the world. 'Miracles' are a return to the primitive 'free' state of creation . . . they express the normal condition of creation before the fall, and still more after Pentecost" (*Orthodox Spirituality,* p. 72). The Orthodox Church has always been an expression of this, and therefore it can be said to be charismatic.

A Prayer to the Holy Spirit

This prayer is included in the daily devotions of Orthodox Christians as well as in many liturgical services:

> O heavenly King, Comforter, the Spirit of Truth, who are everywhere present and fill all things, the Treasury of good things and Giver of life: Come and abide in us, cleanse us from every stain, and save our souls, O Good One.

1 *The Mystical Theology of the Eastern Church,* London, 1957, p. 196.
2 *Christian Initiation and Baptism in the Holy Spirit,* p. 322.
3 Ibid., p. 324.
4 *Orthodox Spirituality,* first published in 1945 by SPCK; this edition, St. Vladimir's Seminary Press, 1978, pp. 62-3.
5 The Episcopal Church of Scotland has always had the Epiclesis in its liturgy, and its Eucharist is the only one in the Anglican Communion which has an Eastern Church feel about it.
6 *Serve the Lord with Gladness,* St. Vladimir's Seminary Press, 1990, p. 51.
7 On this topic a book to study is *In the Light of Christ,* St. Vladimir's Seminary Press, New York, 1986.

8 The Orthodox use this term to describe the work of pioneer missionaries, both men and women, who open up an entirely new part of the world to the gospel.

9 *St. Innocent, Apostle to America,* St. Vladimir's Seminary Press, 1979, p. 83.

16

The True Light

We have seen the true Light; we have received the heavenly Spirit; we have found the true faith, worshipping the undivided Trinity, who has saved us.
The Liturgy of St. John Chrysostom

Holy is the true Light and passing wonderful, lending radiance to them that endured in the heat of the conflict; from Christ they inherit a home of unfading splendour wherein they rejoice with gladness evermore.
The Salisbury Antiphoner

It is an awesome moment. The people of God have received the Holy Gifts of the Body and Blood of Christ. The Liturgy is nearly over. Suddenly the choir bursts out with the words, "We have seen the true light." This ringing chant takes us to the heart of Orthodoxy. The chant goes on, "We have received the heavenly Spirit; we have found the true faith, worshipping the undivided Trinity, who has saved us." Here, joined together in this chant, are five key words which unlock the door of our understanding of Orthodoxy—light, Spirit, faith, Trinity, and salvation.

At this joyful moment we are at the center of Orthodoxy. The Orthodox Church worships and lives in the light and presence of the Trinity. It worships "the true Light which gives light to every man coming into the world" (John 1:9). This is the light that has come into the world, even Jesus Christ. The Orthodox Church worships and receives the heavenly Spirit; Orthodox believers have "found the true faith" and, at great cost in human life, have borne witness to it.

We live in fearful days. Most churches are in serious decline in the Western world. Pascal once wrote, "Men despise religion; they hate it, and fear it is true." He is right, but the other side of the coin is that some *fear it is not true.* It is this fear which lies at least partially behind the tensions which have torn churches apart through the centuries. There has always been a longing for certainty—clear and affirming dogmas to drive away the fear that our faith is unfounded after all. This is the doubt which haunts us. Here, I believe, the Orthodox Church can provide an answer.

How can we be sure about the truth? Is there an outward authority which can provide us with the certainty we deeply desire? The Roman Catholic answer is, "Trust the Church." The evangelical answer is, "Trust the Bible." The Orthodox answer is both of these but adds, "Trust the Holy Spirit."

In 1848 the four Eastern Patriarchs wrote to the Pope to explain how the Orthodox Church understood authority. They declared that the source of authority is not to be found in a single person or hierarch, or even in all the clergy. It is in the entire body of the faithful. Nicholas Zernov adds, "The Orthodox Christians believe that the Holy Spirit guides and protects the Church from all error."[1] It needs to be added that authority is not a matter only for those alive today. The teaching of the saints and Fathers of the Church who have died is part of it. This is what G. K. Chesterton once called "the democracy of the dead."

There is no question that "authority" has been, and still is, the main and ultimate issue which has separated the churches through the centuries—East from West, Protestant from Protestant, Pentecostal from Pentecostal. In the Protestant world the Scriptures, from the Reformation onwards, have been the sure test of doctrinal truth and the provider of certainty and assurance of faith. If the Bible says it, it is certainly true. In the

Roman Catholic world the papacy, and ultimately the Pope himself, are seen as the final authority and the source of certainty—the rock upon which all truth is established. If the Pope says it, you can depend upon it; it is true.

But neither of these sources of authority has delivered the goods. Protestantism has spawned thousands of churches and little "popes," each with their own beliefs and interpretations of biblical truth. Roman Catholicism has its problems with its strict dogmas and authority, especially the dogma of papal infallibility. Is there a way of avoiding the two extremes of papal and biblical infallibility?

The Model of the Jerusalem Council

We need to look at one of the most important stories in the New Testament—the so-called Council of Jerusalem (see Acts 15:1–29). The Church was in danger of being torn apart by a controversy of paramount importance. The decision was bound to affect the whole future of the Church. The issue was whether non-Jews needed to become Jews (the men through circumcision) before they could be baptized as Christians. Saint Paul was adamant; although Jewish himself, he campaigned for the freedom of non-Jewish men and women to become Christian without having to be Jewish first. There were many others who took the opposite position, and Saint Peter wavered between the two, coming down first on one side and then on the other.

So they met in Jerusalem to seek agreement. Although the first Ecumenical Council was not to meet for nearly three hundred years, two main principles were followed at the meeting in Jerusalem. The first was faith in the Holy Spirit as the divine guide to truth, and the second was the consensus of the Church. This was summarized by the definitive words, "For it seemed good to the Holy Spirit, and to us . . ." (Acts 15:28).

At the Council there was full discussion, and both sides

freely put their cases. The Holy Spirit guided them, and the whole leadership of the Church spoke with authority based on confidence in God the Holy Spirit. At this gathering in Jerusalem we find some interesting pointers to what I have just been describing. Let us ask the question, "Why didn't the Apostles settle the matter with a quotation from the lips of Christ?" Would not a "scripture" have been sufficient? One can hardly imagine greater demand for a decisive word from Christ when the whole future mission of the Church was at stake. After all, they knew a great deal more about what Christ said than we have recorded in the Gospels. John Meyendorff has written about this, "Neither side made use of Jesus' sayings on the matter precisely *because there were none,* and nobody proceeded to invent any."[2]

Jesus Christ did not lay down definitive statutes or dogmas to cover every situation, even something as important as this. He did not define the Trinity, describe in detail His two natures, or give His mother the title *Theotokos.* He left the Church to do that. But there is one thing of immense importance that He did do. *He promised the Church the Holy Spirit.* He said to the Apostles, "I still have many things to say to you, but you cannot bear them now. However, when He, the Spirit of truth, has come, He will guide you into all truth. . . . All things that the Father has are Mine. Therefore I said that He [the Holy Spirit] will take of Mine and declare it to you" (John 16:12–15).

But the Church needs to be protected from individual judgment, which has proved one of the most potent causes of division in the Protestant world through the centuries. It is no good someone saying, "The Holy Spirit has revealed this to me." It must also be tested by the Church and compared with the teaching of the Church down the centuries. And the bigger the issue, the wider should be the representation of the Church. In Jerusalem the truth was arrived at through the Holy Spirit *and* the Church. At the Jerusalem Council the Holy Spirit "made it known" to the Church through their representatives, the Apostles and elders. The Holy Spirit did it again at Nicaea in 325 and at the next six Ecumenical Councils. He has continued to do it to this day.

The slogan *sola scriptura* is not enough on its own. The Church always needs the Holy Spirit to guide it in major issues, like defining the Trinity and understanding the Person of Christ, His Incarnation, and the relationship between His humanity and His deity. When the Council ended its sessions the Apostles and elders gave glory to the Holy Spirit, but also affirmed the Church's part in all this. "It seemed good to the Holy Spirit, *and to us,*" they said. The "us" was the whole Church speaking through its representatives. That is made clear when "the apostles and elders, *with the whole church*" (Acts 15:22) chose the emissaries to take the message to the rest of the Church. One cannot see here the authority of one person, a pope or a bishop, however godly or dedicated, for such a vital and universal decision, which affected the whole Church. A Russian lay theologian of the last century called A.S. Khomiakov (1804–60) put it boldly when he wrote, "The Church is not an authority . . . but the Truth." His critique of the whole of Western Christianity was sound. According to him, in the West "authority became external power"—that of the pope or that of the Bible.[3]

The Right Way

The Orthodox Church has helped us to see things that were hidden from us. It has been like strong floodlights turned on, illuminating things we knew before but which we had never seen properly. Two of these are the Feast of the Transfiguration and the Feast of Feasts, Easter—which the Orthodox call Pascha.

Dazzling Light

The Kontakion for the Pre-feast of the Transfiguration wonderfully describes this event: "Today the whole of mortal nature glitters in the divine Transfiguration, in a divine manner, shouting with joy: Christ is transfigured, the Savior of all." Here is a feast which sparkles with the radiance of the glory of God.

As we examine the account of the Transfiguration of Christ on Mount Tabor, as recorded in the Gospels, we discover that most of the major features of Orthodoxy are woven into it. So it is no surprise that the Feast of the Transfiguration has such an important place in Orthodox worship. Its rank is equal to that of Christmas, Theophany (called Epiphany in the West), the Ascension, and Pentecost, yielding in importance only to Easter.

The Orthodox see this event in the life of Christ as a Trinitarian experience, similar to the baptism of Christ, which is remembered on January 6 each year at the Feast of the Theophany. As at Jesus' baptism, there is the voice of the Father, "This is My beloved Son. Hear Him!" (Mark 9:7). This time there is no dove; instead there is the cloud which appears and envelopes them, and in both the Old and New Testaments this often symbolizes the Holy Spirit.

Again when we focus on Christ Himself we see in this incident His two natures, the divine and the human, united and not confused. We see the manhood of Christ, which does not diminish the Godhead. Nothing is taken from His humanity; neither is anything added. In the words of Saint Paul, "in Him dwells all the fullness of the Godhead bodily" (Colossians 2:9). All this was hidden behind the veil of flesh, but for a moment was seen by the three disciples and by Moses and Elijah.

We are in the heartland of Orthodoxy here. For instance, the importance of the communion of saints is underlined by the appearance of Moses and Elijah, talking to Christ. Unlike the Western Church, the Orthodox Church honors Old Testament personalities with the title "saint." And that is not all. Here we also see the Orthodox understanding of "deification," and we observe in Christ's experience the potentiality for our own glorification in Him through the work of the Holy Spirit. Many Orthodox saints have shone physically with the light of God's glory, so that their fellows have had to avert their eyes. Indeed, in traditional Orthodox teaching the Transfiguration has cosmic significance. The light of Christ shines not only from His body, but His clothes and the rocks around are also transfigured. In Mark we are told, "His clothes became shining, exceedingly white, like snow" (Mark 9:3; the Greek is literally "brighter than the sun"). The light of the sun is created light, but Jesus shines with uncreated light. As the kontakion states it, "The whole of mortal nature glitters." The Incarnation is something that not only affects our humanity; potentially it transforms the whole of creation.

There is obviously an important link between this event and the coming events in Jerusalem, Christ's Crucifixion and His Resurrection. According to Saint Luke, this was the subject of the conversation between Jesus and Moses and Elijah (Luke 9:30–32). Thus the Orthodox Church has the Feast of the Elevation of the Cross just forty days after the celebration of the Transfiguration.

An Explosion of Joy

New converts to Orthodoxy will always remember their first Easter or Pascha. Father Dumitru Staniloae writes of Easter as the "center of Orthodox worship." He goes on, "It is an explosion of joy . . . it is the explosion of cosmic joy at the triumph of life." That perfectly describes our experience of our first Pascha Service in 1995 at the Greek Orthodox church in

Bath. It was an "explosion of joy," a "triumph of light."

We have found in the Orthodox Church a sense of "perpetual resurrection" which needs no "bureaucratic protection," as John Betjeman once put it in a poem he wrote after visiting an Orthodox church in Greece. The sense of timelessness in Orthodoxy is part of this living resurrection. How time-oriented we Westerners have become! I found a marvelous antidote to this when I became an Orthodox priest: when we serve the Divine Liturgy we wear on our wrists cuffs which hide our watches.

An unknown Soviet prisoner in a Siberian labor camp, imprisoned for his Orthodox faith, once wrote a letter describing Easter. On Easter Day in this gulag there were no services, no bells, no candles, and no special Easter dishes. In fact, there was deliberately *more* work and *more* interference than usual. There was more spying and there were more threats from the secret police. "Yet Easter was there," he wrote, "great, holy, spiritual, unforgettable. It was blessed by the presence of our risen God among us—blessed by the silent Siberian stars and by our sorrows. . . . Death is conquered, fear no more, an eternal Easter is given to us!"[4] It is that "eternal Easter," experienced by a Russian imprisoned in Siberia for his faith, that has been our great gain. It is what the true light of the Orthodox Church has given us. As Orthodox we live from one Easter to the next.

"Christ is Risen!"
"He is risen indeed!"

1 *The Concise Encyclopaedia of Living Faiths,* Hutchinson, p. 100.

2 John Meyendorff, *Living Tradition,* St. Vladimir's Seminary Press, 1978, p. 34.

3 The paper from which this quote comes was published in French in

1872 (Lausanne and Vevey) pp. 3–7. It is quoted in Meyendorff, *Living Tradition,* p. 27f.

4 Bishop Kallistos Ware, *The Orthodox Way,* p. 117.

Select Bibliography

Coniaris, Anthony, *Introducing the Orthodox Church,* Light and Life, 1982

Ware, Timothy, *The Orthodox Church,* Penguin Books, 1963; latest edition 1993

Ware, Kallistos, *The Orthodox Way,* St. Vladimir's Seminary Press, 1993

Clément, Olivier, *The Roots of Christian Mysticism,* New City, 1993

Gillet, Lev, *Orthodox Spirituality,* SPCK, 1945; new edition, St. Vladimir's Seminary Press, 1978

Gillquist, Peter, *Becoming Orthodox,* Conciliar Press, 1989

Gillquist, Peter (ed.), *Coming Home,* Conciliar Press, 1992

Harakas, Stanley, *455 Questions and Answers,* Light and Life, 1987

Ignatius, Patriarch, *The Resurrection and Modern Man,* St. Vladimir's Seminary Press, 1985

Moore, Lazarus, *St. Seraphim of Sarov,* New Sarov Press, 1994

Schmemann, Alexander, *Great Lent,* St. Vladimir's Seminary Press, 1990

All the books listed are normally available through Conciliar Press.
Please call (831) 336-5118 for current availability and price information.